Personal–Injury Lawyers

America's Shame

by

Anton Androv (victim)

Copyright, 2024, Anton Androv

All rights reserved. Printed in the United States of America. This publication is protected by Copyright and permission should be obtained from the author prior to any reproduction, storage in retrieval system, or in transmission in any form by any means, electronic, mechanical, photocopying, and recording or likewise. For information regarding permission(s) contact the author through the publisher.

Dedication

This book is dedicated to Michael Herring Esq., the only lawyer who tried to help me.

Acknowledgements

This book would not be possible without the help of key individuals: my sons Steven and Michael who helped with the analysis of fraudulent videos, Lynne who typed difficult to read manuscript, Ann Marie who did the cover design and editing, my colleague Mark who put everything together and edited it on the computer, and attorney Michael H for legal guidance. They were a great team and I thank them.

Content

Chapter 1 America's problem – one lawyer for every 11 people

Chapter 2 The incident – an accident fraud at Disney World

Chapter 3 The insurance company trauma- the reason for "Don-got-me's"

Chapter 4 The 3-month Investigation trip – trying to resolve the incident

Chapter 5 Thrown under the bus – Death by insurance company

Chapter 6 The Disney Dilemma – no help from Mickey

Chapter 7 The law enforcement dilemma – no help from police

Chapter 8 The insurance company dilemma – they can be you adversary

Chapter 9 The lawyer dilemma – no injury, no lawyer

Chapter 10 Solving the Don-got-me problem – try prayer

Epilogue – What is a driver to do in an accident?

Preface

The closest that people are to death is probably driving an automobile in traffic. A fraction of a second distraction can lead to a collision with another vehicle and possible injury or death. I recently came as close to death at the wheel as I have ever been. I was heading to another city on a short business trip on a four lane divided interstate toll way at 65 miles per hour. It was a clear day with summer weather conditions and the toll way was busy, but not overly busy. When I was approaching an entrance to the toll way, I noticed a line of tail-gating cars (maybe 5 or 6) heading onto the toll way. I intuitively touched my brake to disconnect my cruise control and started to slow down. Unfortunately, the car in front of me (about 500 feet) did not slow for the toll way entrance and his 65 MPH vehicle suddenly encountered a "train" of entering vehicles at 50 or so MPH. He swerved left to avoid the cars entering our travel lane and ended up in the grass median and without stopping he made a u turn and headed across my travel lane for the right shoulder of the road. His car was perpendicular to mine in my travel lane. I stopped completely and he missed me by a few feet.

This was the closest that I have ever come to a high speed collision in my 60 plus years of driving. The point that pertains to this book is that according to Google (and they are omniscient), all vehicle drivers will be involved with from 1 to 4 accidents in there driving lives. And most of us (including moi), are not prepared for what happens in a crash. This book is about my being rear-ended by a tourist shuttle bus on its way from a hotel to Disney World in Florida. I did everything concerning this event wrong and I lost my trust in the institutions that are supposed to protect us. The bus company submitted a fraudulent dash cam video to my insurance company. They did this because they knew that once you get an insurance company to accept blame, you can contact a Don-got-me lawyer to get a lifetime of riches for faked injuries.

This book presents specific steps for everyone to take in the event of a vehicle crash: what to do at the scene, what to do about law enforcement, what to do about insurance, and what to do about lawyers. In my case I also had to deal with a foreign government: Disney World. Who knew that the United States of America has a sovereign nation in the middle of Florida? They can do anything that they want regarding public safety; they are exempt from all USA public safety laws. Who knew?

There are ten chapters in this book. The first five chapters chronicle the events surrounding my rear-ending on Disney property: what happened, trying to get law enforcement involved, trying to get a lawyer, trying to get Florida to enforce its accident fraud law, and how my insurance company became my ultimate adversary. There is a chapter on "the Disney Dilemma", what they did to me; there is a chapter on the law enforcement dilemma, how nobody at any government level would even talk with me; there is a chapter on the insurance company dilemma; there is a reason why auto insurance company TV ads are humorous skits with no substance. The last dilemma chapter is on the Don-got-me lawyers; I believe them to be the root cause of accident fraud and an existential threat to America. They know that they have a guaranteed win against any insurance company. That is why they advertise lottery-like winnings to young healthy people. All they have to do is claim that their client has lower-back pain, trauma, or some other injury that cannot be medically measured. This chapter is followed by a chapter on what can be done to curb Don-got-me behavior on the part of lawyers. Don-got-me lawyers cost every person who pays for auto insurance an estimated $500 to $1000 dollars a year extra to cover insurance company losses to them. You are also paying for their incessant ads with your monthly auto insurance bill.

The book closes with an epilogue with a checklist of what to do in the event of a vehicle crash. What you have been told to do by insurance companies and government agencies is what cost me my life and possessions. You need to do what this book suggests. Overall, America has a very, very serious problem. We have more lawyers per capita than any country in the world and a civilization based upon litigation is not sustainable. Suing each other should not be the 4th largest industry in the USA. The auto insurance industry is around a 400 billion dollar industry, and it does not produce any food, clothing, or shelter for its customers. (The US meat industry is 294B; the apparel industry is 180B, and the new-home industry is 132B). However, it does provide great wealth for Don-got-me lawyers. There are ways to fix the problem. This book makes suggestions to elected officials. It is a must read for all who drive an automobile in the USA. You will have an accident in your lifetime and it can take all that you have if you respond wrongly like I did.

    A. Androv

Chapter 1
America's Problem

Introduction

Whatever you do, whatever you make, whatever you say, there is a pack of soulless lawyers who want to take everything that you have, to shut down your company, to stop your medical treatment, so that they can get incredible jury awards by suing you for whatever you do. Today's Wall Street Journal contained an article about a 1.7 billion jury award over a truck rollover accident. The truck manufacturer did not make the roof strong enough to resist a rollover. Next week it will be a 2-billion dollar suit because the company's bumpers were not strong enough to deflect a 60-mph head-on collision. Today on TV, Smith and Smith (or whatever their name was) Attorneys played ads every five minutes telling people if they have lung cancer to go to them because they know how to blame your lung cancer on the local power plants who used asbestos in their facilities many years ago.

Companies are put out of business daily because something hurt somebody and they did not have a warning on the product about what hurt somebody using their products. Currently one of the few remaining manufacturing companies in the USA is being put out of business by lawsuits from US military veterans. Some have diminished hearing allegedly because they used the company's foam earplugs during shooting events and the earplugs did not prevent hearing loss. This is absurd. If you can still hear anything when wearing ear protection, it is not protecting. I can still hear wearing my $400, noise-canceling headphones. No hearing protection devices stop all vibration to hearing sensors. Everybody knows this. They reduce the level of sound to the hearing sensors. Some device or system like a sound-recording studio would be needed to completely shield noise and such equipment is certainly not compatible with a military situation.

It is not possible to anticipate and warn about everything possible on every component of every product. The United States' legal system is out of control. According to a lawyer friend (who I believe) there is a lawyer for every eleven people in the USA. Google's answer is more like one per one thousand people, but we only have one medical doctor to every 16,000 people. According to Google, the average salary of lawyers in the USA is $126,000 per year, and there are 1.3 million lawyers in the US. Thus, between 100 and 200 billion dollars of litigation profit is needed per year to feed and clothe lawyers and their families. The size of the litigation industry is probably about ½ trillion dollars per year. And it produces no product to support our civilization, no roads, no food, and no infrastructure.

Throughout recorded history there have always been two classes of humans: the elite and the non-elite; the non-elite were most of the population. Archeologists who uncover ruins of dead civilizations note these two-level civilizations just about everywhere. There has to be a leadership for a civilization to exist, but leadership does not have to have all of the wealth and the better living conditions (houses and possessions). But historically the elite had the wealth and power. America's lawyers are our society's elite.

Thus, the root cause of USA litigious society is the high number of lawyers. A civilization has evolved that has suing others for their possessions, the goal of life. If something bad befalls you or any family member, we hire a lawyer to sue somebody with wealth. Taking the wealth of others is judged to negate the effects of the bad thing that happened.

My first exposure to America's world of litigation occurred shortly after I graduated from college. I was called to jury duty. A doctor, an obstetrician, was being sued for injury to a newborn through the use of forceps during delivery. When I was being vetted by the lawyers, it was learned that the doctor being sued was my wife's obstetrician. He delivered our oldest son. My wife thought him to be the best doctor ever. Forceps at that time (1960's) were widely used in delivery, but still her doctor was being sued for using them. Why? Because a lawyer can convince a jury of just about anything if he or she is skilled in the craft of selecting jury members that can be easily swayed. Most of the US population watched a jury set free a famous football player who we all knew murdered his wife. A master-of-his-craft lawyer convinced the jury that the killer was innocent because he struggled to put on a leather glove found at the crime scene. It may have been rained on and shrunk. Juries are putty in the hands of a crafty trial lawyer and huge awards for absurd events are commonplace. As I write this, my city awarded four million dollars to a firefighter who was forced to attend a Juneteenth party that offered Kentucky Fried Chicken as part of the celebration's food offerings. He became so distressed at this that he can no longer work as a firefighter and he will use his four million dollars to care for his distress. That award was paid by local taxpayers.

It is the purpose of this book to recount an accident that is in the same vein as the Kentucky Fried Chicken. I was stopped in stop-and-go traffic in a rented 2900-pound Honda HR-V when I was rear ended by a 40,000 pound 60-passenger tour bus. The damage to the Honda was about what one would get when a shopping cart blows into the side of a car. Of course, there was no damage to the bus's massive rubber bumper. However, the bus driver concocted a video of me hitting him and that he sustained lifelong injury that can only be fixed by suing me, the auto rental company, and my insurance company for whatever my insurance company would allow.

The objective of this book is to try to show United State citizens that we as a nation are tolerating a legal system that is an existential threat to our civilization. A half a trillion dollars (per National Safety Council) a year for lawyers and jury awards is not sustainable. Our civilization will fail.

Nobody will want to run a business or make a product or grow food knowing that at any second, something wrong may happen to somebody and we the producers will lose everything by lawsuit. Why try to succeed when if you do you will be sued to death by the trial lawyers who can get anything that they want from a jury.

The book chronicles my fight to prove my innocence: dealing with the insurance company, dealing with lawyers, dealing with law enforcement, trying to communicate with political leaders, dealing with attorney generals, and dealing with rogue corporations. The book ends with "the results of my fight" and what the USA should do to save our civilization from death by litigation.

The plaintiff

Who am I and why am I writing this? I am an old person who continues to work past typical retirement age. I am a materials engineer specializing in the field of tribology: the study of interacting surfaces and friction, wear, lubrication and related subjects. I retired on a Friday from a corporate job after thirty-eight years and started working at my son's company on the following Monday. I am still working there after twenty-one years.

Mostly I work on self-funded fundamental research. I develop wear and friction tests and then work to make them international standards. When I started this job, we were building test machines for sale. Now we mostly offer testing services. I usually attend two meetings each year on standardization of tests and I attend one or two technical conferences a year. I try to present at least one paper a year at one of these conferences.

This book will present the details of an accident scam that I fell into in going to a technical conference at a Disney World hotel in the Orlando area. There are chapters on the various aspects of the accident scam, but the underlying purpose of this book is to tell the people who run the United States, (there are about 600 e.g. congress, judges, cabinet members, etc.) that they need to do something immediately to curtail the litigation frenzy that is smothering our civilization. I maintain homes in New York State and in Florida. In both locations there are billboards on every major highway showing big pictures of attractive young, healthy people stating "Don got me $600,000". The TV news in both locations have lawyers showing people saying, "Don got me 1.3 million, Don got me 2.6 million, Don got me 3 million."

The advertising is incessant. It has driven me to not watch any TV. The lawyer billboards make driving anyplace in the USA unpleasant. Why do Don-got-me lawyers do this? They do this because it works. They convince everyday people that they can become wealthy if they sue somebody with deep pockets. These ads show that you can be healthy and unharmed and still get millions from accident lawsuits. Lots of the TV ads show very pretty young women claiming: "Don got me 2.3 million". They indoctrinate the public in suing even though there is nothing physically wrong with you. All persons can claim a lower back injury because it is not medically possible to prove that your back does not hurt. You can claim that your back hurts at all times from any accident and all of the medical people in the world cannot disprove it. Lawyers know this; that is why they can claim to always win your case and make you (and them) wealthy. They take a third or more of any insurance or jury award.

I became the victim of a Don-got-me lawyer scam, a faked accident, and a faked injury. I tried everything possible to show that the event was a scam; I learned that there is no help available from law enforcement or from your insurance company. Individuals in both organizations get paid when you get entrapped in a fraudulent accident scam. Police officers do not care that you are getting sued by a faked accident. Unfortunately, I learned that my insurance company works the same. Accident investigators get paid whether the accident was fraudulent or not. They just want to settle and do not care that an accident is fraudulent.

I never realized how existential the Don-got-me lawyer problem was until I became a victim. This book is a detailed account of my victimization, and I will present guidelines to follow in all vehicle accidents to prevent victimization like mine. Tables 1 and 2 present some facts about accidents and the auto insurance industry that relate to this book. This book will show the world what a bad insurance company looks like and what readers should know about screening insurance companies before committing to one.

The objective of this book is to have the 600 people who control the USA (the president, the cabinet, congress and the Supreme Court Justices) develop legislation to reign in accident fraud, capricious lawsuits (trauma distress etc.), non-involvement of law enforcement in vehicle accidents, and legislation to allow insurance company customers a voice in deciding accident fault. Overall, America's litigious society is ending our civilization. America cannot exist as a country with Don-got-me lawyers offering a life of wealth to anybody who fakes an injury.

Country	number of citizens per lawyer	population
USA	248	330,000,000
Peoples Republic of China	45,000	1,300,000,000
Russia	2040	145,000,000
India	1108	1,440,000,000
France	1220	65,000,000

England   68,000,000
                465
Indonesia   277,000,000
                12043

Table 1 The number of citizens per lawyer in various countries (from various sources)

1. The average American driver will be in 1 to 4 accidents in their lifetime.
2. There are about 6 million auto accidents in the USA per year and about 13 percent have medically reported injuries.
3. About 13 percent of automobile drivers in the USA drive without auto insurance.
4. Ninety four percent of all auto accident claims are settled without court action.
5. The average 30-second TV commercial costs at least $500.
6. The average billboard ad costs about $2500/month
7. Police respond to less than 10 percent of all USA auto accidents (per US Department of Justice, NCJ 253 739)
8. The average auto "injury" award is $18,000 (John Foy Associates)
9. There are no medical measurements to verify many alleged "injuries", like: trauma, stress, mood, uncomfortable, angst, sadness, anxiety, nervousness, apprehension, distress, pain, hardship, fear, suffering, etc.
10. Money awarded by a court satisfies any injury, wrongful death, any wrong, any

altercation, any contract, any cause of a lawsuit (per lawyers).

Table 2 Facts related to automobile accidents (from Google and other sources)

Why you should care about Don-got-me lawyers

Epidemic lawsuits cost every person in the USA, especially automobile owners. If you pay $3000 per year for your auto insurance, about $1000 is your contribution to Don-got-me lawyers. US automobile owners paid about 460 billion dollars in premiums in 2022. There are about 1.3 million Lawyers in the USA and they have an average salary of $126,000. Thus we the people have to come up with $160 billion dollars to pay their salaries. This is my basis for stating that one third of your insurance premium goes to paying Don-go-me lawyers.

The incomprehensible part of this situation is that the Don-go-me lawyers, the ones with the TV and billboard ads, obtain their wealth by enticing anyone involved in any auto accident, no matter how minor, to sue the other person's insurance company. Their message is:

If you claim an injury, even if it is anxiety, we will obtain a large sum of money for you.

Unfortunately, it is true that they will get a win over any insurance company. My incident showed me that insurance companies are no match for trial lawyers. My insurance company came across to me as contemptuous to clients, impotent in defending clients, and in general, incompetent in technical matters related to car crashes. Insurance companies will not challenge a Don-got-me lawyer. They charge enough in premiums to just pay any lawsuits brought by the Don-got-me's. This is why the Don-got-me lawyers boast:

I will get you paid!

There is no contest. Auto insurance companies lack the skills to do anything about accident fraud. Who knew? What I learned about my insurance company in my incident explains all of the ads that I see from insurance companies on TV. One large company advertises with humorous scenes involving a lizard. One company shows a group of buffoons wearing white uniforms doing stupid things. Another company produces humorous skits on a waterfront with the Statue of Liberty in the background. One famous auto insurance company for years constantly played an ad showing a man sitting on a couch in the middle of a heavily traveled highway as the reason why you should buy insurance from them. Another auto insurance company shows an angry man with a bandage on his face destroying other people's property as the basis for buying their insurance. We are offered funny skits to use as the basis of selection of an auto insurance purveyor. I believe that they do not want to admit that they do not have distinguishing properties and practices to offer to consumers. We have to buy auto insurance by law, so give them whatever amuses them. That seems to be the attitude of the insurance companies. Most people have only one or two accidents in their lifetime; thus, most people will not know about their insurance company's lack of skills to deal with Don-got-me lawyers.

I learned many things from my rear-ending about lawyers, about insurance companies, about law enforcement and about Disney World, and I hope that my sharing of these learnings will help the average automobile owner make right decisions with regard to an accident and with regard to selecting an insurance company. I did everything wrong and I paid for it with my life and possessions. The inability of insurance companies and the USA court system to deal with what the Don-got-me lawyers are doing creates an existential problem that needs to be addressed by Americas elected leaders. Consumers also need to ponder why insurance companies offer up silly skits as the basis for your $3000 or more per year. Do you want to buy insurance from the company with the silliest ad? Are they telling consumers that they have insufficient intellect to select an insurance company on the basis of benefits and service?

Civilizations by definition require people to participate in the things that comprise a civilization: people living in proximity with others, people protecting each other, people caring for each other, people making useful things, people buying these things, people offering services to others, etc.

Sustaining a civilization requires continuing effort on the part of the people that make up the civilization. Most of the civilizations that have existed on Planet Earth have ceased to exist because of some event, change, or practice. The incredible Egyptian pharaonic civilization ceased to exist after more than 3000 years of continuous existence. Ancient Greece was an incredible civilization in scope and accomplishments. It disappeared after about 500 years of success. The Roman Empire was the most progressive civilization that the world has ever known. It only lasted in the west about 500 years. The United States is an infant civilization compared to these others; will it last another century? In 2023, most Americans are unsure about the fate of our civilization. Factions are the main problem. We have too many. The main economic problem is: "nobody works". Free things from government brought this condition about. The Don-got-me problem is that these people are promoting using lawsuits as the path to wealth and happiness. This is a situation that is incommensurate with the sustainability of USA's civilization. Something must be done by legislation or conversion, of Don-got-me lawyers or the USA will go the way of Pharaonic Egypt, Classic Greece, and The Roman Empire.

Don-got-me lawyers are a significant threat to America's civilization

Chapter 2
The Incident

Most of us never give a second thought to driving someplace: to work, to the store, shopping, whatever. We never think that we will be hit by another car or that we will hit another car. We have confidence in our driving. In fact, confidence behind the wheel is key to being able to drive, (along with physical attributes like good vision and reactions).

Overall, driving an automobile is the most dangerous thing that most people will ever do. On a highway you are often a split second away from death to yourself or to others. It only takes an instant to make a fatal mistake. However, confidence in our acquired driving skills allows us to not concern ourselves with the consequences of a wrong decision or movement of the vehicle's controls.

It is the purpose of this chapter to recount a driving incident on one of my technical conference trips that was life changing for me and should be life changing for all vehicle drivers who read about my incident. The chapter objective is to educate all drivers on what should be done in the event of any vehicle-to-vehicle accident. I did not do what I should have, and I paid dearly for that.

The chapter starts with the incident situation, where I was, what I was doing; then discusses the incident, then the immediate aftermath; the ensuing insurance company issues will be a separate chapter.

The situation

The technical conference that I attended had to do with tribology research (the science of contacting surfaces).

One of my principal technical societies has an annual meeting in the spring they have their conferences in large hotels and they usually have about 1500 attendees and several hundred oral paper presentations. I was scheduled to give two papers on the second day of the conference. The conference was held at a hotel that was within the Disney World complex near Orlando, Florida.

When I learned that my papers were approved for presentation, I made plans to stay at the small house I own in an Orlando suburb and drive to the Disney hotel daily. It was about a sixty-mile drive. Paper presenters are required to attend a speaker's breakfast the day of their paper to meet the other speakers and the session chair. The speakers' breakfast was at 7:00 AM. I knew that traffic would be very heavy in and around Orlando on work-day mornings so I decided to stay at the conference hotel the night before my talk. I would not have to fight rush hour traffic to get to the hotel by 6:45 AM.

However, the conference hotel was fully booked, and I was given a room in an overflow hotel on International Drive. I knew where it was. The conference started on Sunday with registration and a cocktail reception. I flew into Orlando on Saturday afternoon, rented a small car (Honda HRV) and drove to my house. Sunday afternoon I drove to the conference hotel to find out where it was located, where to park, to see the presentation rooms, and in general, familiarize myself with the entire venue. I Googled directions and maps to locate the conference hotel. Disney's main Disney World attraction is their Magic Kingdom. Disney has a four-lane divided expressway leading to a giant parking lot that serves the Magic Kingdom called One World Drive. It is the only way to access the Magic Kingdom and my conference hotel and other resorts are off this main road.

It was very difficult to find the conference hotel, but it was high with a unique feature on the roof that I could use to find the place. I located the hotel successfully on Sunday, learned where to park, and I registered at the conference and drove back to my house in the Orlando suburb. Monday morning, I drove to the hotel on International Drive. They had shuttles to take conference delegates to the conference hotel. I took one in the morning and left my rental car at the overflow hotel. In the morning I took a 6:30 shuttle to my speakers'' breakfast and spent the day at the conference. At 6:00 PM I took the shuttle back to the hotel and drove to my house in the rental car.

The incident

The conference talks started at 8:30 AM on Wednesday. My plan was to get there at that time.

I left my house at 7:00AM figuring that I could make the sixty-mile drive in an hour and make the 8:30 start of the talks. I left my house at 7:00 and took a tollway that pretty much ends at Disney's entrance road: One World Drive.

Traffic was very heavy near the Orlando airport and I had to stop six times to pay tolls. (I paid cash). I exited the tollway about 8:15 and within about three minutes I entered Disney's One World Drive. About a mile or two on One World Drive I encountered a barricade of sawhorses across One World Drive. There were no people or other cars around, no signs, no detours. However, the barricade was at a road that intersected from the right. I turned right on it. It wandered through woods and clusters of buildings. I saw a sign for Disney Wilderness Park or some such thing. I do not know how long I spent on this circuitous path, but I became very concerned that I was totally lost. I just kept driving. There were no people any place, no stores, no anything. It was absolutely deserted. Finally, I spotted an intersecting road. I had no idea what the road was or where it went, but I headed for it. When I arrived at the intersection, I found a huge confluence of paving and grass medians. There were no traffic controls at the intersection, but I stopped to assess the situation. I saw two lanes of bumper-to-bumper traffic heading to my right in stop and go fashion. There was a grass median about twenty feet wide separating the clogged lanes from two lanes that were empty. No traffic at all.

I really had no choice on what to do. I had to follow the flow of stop and go traffic because my chances of making it to the empty lanes were nil. I would have to go perpendicular to two lanes of cars intent on going wherever the road went. My rationale on driving into the mayhem was that there may be a live person someplace along the path of the stop and go traffic that I can stop and ask where I am.

I started to carve my way into the first lane of stop and go. I made it. Almost instantly after I made it into the first lane of stop and go, an opening occurred in the second lane. I drove for it. I made it into the opening, but then the lane of traffic stopped. I stopped as well. I was still on maybe a 60-degree angle to the traffic flow. As I waited for the stopped traffic to restart, I felt the rear end of my rental car (a little HRV Honda) get pushed sideways. There was no noise, no impact (I later learned that the bus had a huge rubber bumper).

I had no idea what transpired. I put my car in park with the engine still running and opened the driver side door to see what the side push was all about. As I opened my door, I saw a huge sixty-passenger bus back away from my rear fender, pulling off a strip of rubber that surrounded the rear driver-side wheel well. The bus just sat there running. Nobody came out of the bus. I went back to my car and drove it about ten feet to get it straight in my lane of traffic. The bus then backed across both lanes of traffic. All traffic on this side of the highway was stopped. After about five minutes a man emerged from the bus holding a cell phone horizontal at his mouth and talking into it. I assumed it was the bus driver. He ignored me. He was talking intensely to somebody on his phone. He paced back and forth in front of the bus as he talked on the phone.

The front door was opened on the bus. I stepped inside briefly and saw passengers on both sides of the aisle. I did not stay on the bus long enough to count passengers. Then I went in my car and got my Daytimer (calendar) and decided to get the license plate and name of the bus recorded. I did so. The driver was still talking on his phone. Finally, he talked with me. He asked if I wanted the police and I said yes. He went back on his phone. After about five minutes he said, "The police are not coming." I asked for his insurance company name, license and the like and I gave him my business card. He did not respond to my request.

Then a car came down the empty side of the divided highway and stopped by the bus. It was Disney security person in a car labeled "Disney Security". He immediately asked the bus driver and me to exchange vehicle information and get the vehicle out of the traffic lanes. Cars were now backed up for miles.

However, before I responded to the security person's request for an exchange of vehicle information I asked where I was. I told him how I ran into a barricade on One World Drive heading to the Dolphin Hotel and I took the only other road option, but I do not know where I am at this point. He told me that I was back on One World Drive and

I was about one-half mile from the entrance to the Magic Kingdom parking lot. And the steady stream of vehicles is for the Magic Kingdom. The park probably opens at 9:00 AM and it was probably 8:30 or so, but I did not look at my watch. I was in a complete state of shock over what happened.

The bus driver was back on the phone. He got on the bus and moved it a few more times. Finally, he came out of the bus and the security person went to his vehicle and showed us a form to fill out. It was a State of Florida accident form to record the details of both vehicles. He gave it to us on a clipboard so we could fill it out immediately. I filled out my portion. He tried to get the bus driver to fill out his portion but he resisted. Then he asked the bus driver to move the bus and allow one lane of traffic to flow. The bus driver moved the bus and came out again.

I had the clipboard now and I tried to fill out the form with information that I got verbally from the bus driver. He had an accent and I did not understand him so I asked him to write in his name and company etc. He scribbled something on the form, but I could not read it. Then he handed the clipboard back to me and said he had to go now. He got in his bus and left. My car was still blocking a travel lane. I asked the Disney security person how to get to the Dolphin Hotel and he told me to make a U-turn at the next opening in the road median and head back a mile or two where there would be signs for the hotel. I put the rubber strip that the bus pulled off my car in the back seat and drove off. There was no damage to my vehicle that would affect driving. There were two dents in the rear door and the torn rubber strip around the wheel well. There was no damage at all to the massive rubber bumper on the bus.

I arrived at my conference hotel a little after 9:00. I parked the car right at the front door since I was so upset with what happened. I got hit by a bus because Disney closed the road to the resort without giving users of the only road a detour or instructions of what to do about its closed road. Without a doubt Disney caused this accident.

The immediate aftermath

I attended talks all day and left the hotel for my Florida house about 6:00 PM. Incredible as it may seem I was concerned that the bus driver could get fired for rear-ending me. In the morning I skipped conference talks and went to the city police department to ask if I could get a police report or something from the police. There were two women behind a glass wall to talk to. I told one that I wanted to talk about the incident with a police officer. She asked where the incident happened. I replied, "at Disney World". Her immediate response was, "That is out of our jurisdiction" and she would not call in a police officer. I asked them whose jurisdiction is it. She told me she didn't know, but it was not theirs. I left disgusted.

Next, I drove to the airport where I rented the car and told the rental company agent that I was rear-ended. She gave me a detailed accident form to fill out. I asked if anybody wanted to see the damage. She said, "No, just fill out the form and return it when you return the car on Sunday" (it was Thursday). I had an early flight out and at this airport the rental companies are closed before 8:00 AM. You just leave the car in a designated parking lot and put the keys in a drop box.

The rental car accident form said to contact your insurance company if you didn't have their insurance. I always use my insurance since the rental insurance is often more than the cost of the car rental. I called my insurance company and they gave a claim number over the phone.

Next, I decided to get estimates on the car repair. I knew of a large nationwide collision shop on a highway I often use. I went there to ask for a damage estimate. She told me that she could give me a time at 2 PM a week from next Tuesday. Who knew? Booking a dent quote is like getting a tee time at an exclusive golf course.

My city has a street full of new car dealerships, so I decided to shop big dealers. Most have collision shops. The first new car dealer that I encountered on the auto dealer road had a huge separate building for collision work. I went there. Somebody came out as soon as I pulled up to tell me where to park to get the damage assessed. I showed the person the detached rubber strip and the door dents and he said that it would be about a $2000 repair. He then told me where to pull over and someone would inspect it in detail and give me a written estimate. After about twenty minutes a person came out with a clipboard and started taking photos all over the car and damaged door. Then he told me to go to a waiting room. He came to the waiting room with a detailed repair quotation. It was four pages long and typed- very professional. His estimate was about $4000. The parts are very expensive. The rubber strip was $800 a hubcap was $500. (My insurance company eventually paid the rental car company $750 for damages).

I stopped my incident follow-up at this point. I figured that the insurance company would handle everything. They will contact the bus company that rear-ended me and the bus company's insurance company will pay for the rental car repairs.

What happened next?

I returned to my home up north and never really thought about the incident. I had somebody hit my rental car years ago in Hilton Head, NC and my insurance company handled everything. This time I received a call from my insurance company about three weeks after the incident. It was from a person in a city about sixty miles from my home. The person on the phone was curt and rude. He asked me to tell him what happened and that my phone conversation was being recorded. I recounted how I was rear-ended by a bus while stopped in stop and go traffic. I probably talked for three or four minutes. He asked me a few questions that I do not recall and my phone interview was ended by the insurance company person.

About two weeks later, I got a letter in the mail from my insurance company stating that they and the rental car company are being sued by a personal injury lawyer on behalf of the bus driver. They stated in the letter that my coverage limit was $300,000. Of course, I took this to mean that they will make me personally responsible for any settlement- the $300.000.

I interpreted this letter to mean that I am involved in a scam on the part of the bus company and bus driver. There was no damage to the bus, two door dents and a missing piece of rubber trim on my rental car and nobody got hurt because there was no impact and besides, I was stopped and hit by the bus.

However, the bus driver's strange behavior at the scene was starting to make sense. He was on the phone and moving the bus all over the place for about a half-hour and he refused to give me his name and insurance information. I also looked over the bus closely to see if there were any signs of damage to the bus at all. The bus was big, at least sixty passengers. It had a massive black rubber front bumper. I looked at the corner of the bumper where he hit my rear wheel. All that happened was a mark on the bumper where accumulated road dust was removed. There was no paint on the rubber from my car, no rubber damage at all, only some road dirt removed.

The bus driver certainly was not injured. He was pacing back and forth on his phone and getting back into the bus and moving it about. He had no impairment and a Disney security person could testify to this. The Disney security person tried patiently to get the bus driver to exchange insurance information with me and stop blocking the two lanes of traffic leading to the Magic Kingdom.

Incredibly, when I left the incident scene, I said to myself that I hoped that the poor bus driver doesn't get fired for rear-ending me. Little did I know that the "poor bus driver" was going to become rich by stealing money from me, my insurance company and the rental car company? The letter on my insurance limit signaled to me that this is going to be the fight of my life.

Chapter 3
The Insurance Company Trauma

The liability-limit letter from my insurance company initiated a substantial letter writing and investigation campaign on my part. However, shortly after my insurance company assigned an investigator, I got a call from somebody in my insurance company saying that the bus company has all of their buses fitted with dash-cams and that they are sending a video of the incident. My insurance company investigator was beyond rude at this point and I vowed to never speak with him again. I sent a registered letter to the CEO of the insurance company in New York City to that effect. He did respond to my letter by making the claims investigator's boss, a woman in Florida, my insurance company contact. She was at least professional in demeanor.

The video

It was about this time that she sent me a copy of the video that supposedly come off of the bus dash-cam. The incident video was attached to an email sent to me by my insurance company. The video started with a scene showing a vehicle on a divided highway (two lanes in each direction separated by a grassy median). The video showed a time in one corner and a speed of 30 mph in another. The video is allegedly being made by a dash-cam on the bus that rear-ended my vehicle. The bus is in the left lane and only two vehicles are shown in the right lane, both about ¼ mile ahead. The bus approaches and passes the first vehicle and then passes the second vehicle which was the same model (a Honda CRV) as my rental car, but a different color. As the bus approaches the Honda, it signals to move from the right lane to a position in front of the bus. There are flashes of the hood of the Honda in view of the das-cam and then the video stops with the Honda stopped in the left lane with a piece of something hanging from the left of the vehicle. The length of the video was 23 seconds and it was fabricated to imply that the Honda on the highway was my vehicle and that I sideswiped the bus.

My initial reaction to the video was that it was absurd. It showed that it was a video of somebody's desktop computer screen not the output of a dash-cam. I thought that this was so crude that it should not be accepted by anybody as authentic. I could easily see how it was fabricated and that everybody knows that videos can be seamlessly made to show anything. During the past US presidential election, I was sent scores of videos showing candidate Biden doing everything from riding a camel to hugging Ruth Bader Ginsburg. They looked authentic. Cutting and pasting along with Photoshop allows this to be the case. Surely the insurance company knows this and would reject this attempt to defraud the insurance company by blaming me for getting rear-ended by a bus. Au contraire, I get an email from the insurance company saying that they believed the video and that I sideswiped the bus.

The bus company

One of my first defensive actions was to send in the accident form required by the state of Florida. I got the forms on line, but I did not have the necessary information on the bus that rear-ended me. I was not able to get the name, address, license number, vehicle owner and insurance company. The bus drove off without giving me this information. The bus driver scribbled some illegible writing on the form given to us by the insurance company, but it did not really contain the bus driver's name. It had the name of an insurance company. I Googled it and it was a house in Tampa with a sign out front saying "insurance agent". I got the bus license number when the driver was walking about on his cell phone. I also got the name of the bus company from a small sign on the side of the bus. I Googled the bus company and Google said that the bus company was owned by a politician in the Philippines. They operate similar to a limousine service, shuttling tourists from hotels to Orlando attractions.

I was able to get the bus driver's name, but no address for the insurance company. My insurance company also gave me a name of the bus's insurance company. It was different from the name given me by the bus driver. As of this writing, I have not investigated the bus company's insurance company. It was a name that I never heard of. In any case, I was able to submit a completed accident form to the state of Florida by their law.

State of Florida Notification

My first action in getting law enforcement involved was a letter to the Governor of Florida. I tried to get the police to come to the accident scene, but the bus driver said that he called and that they would not come because the incident happened on Disney property. My letter to the governor asked for government help because law enforcement will not enforce laws on Disney property. Disney World in Florida is like having a North Korea between Orlando and Tampa. This is forbidden territory to law enforcement.

The Florida legislature in 2021 or 2022 voted to dissolve Disney World's separate country status, but dissolution will take years. This being the case, I asked the governor if he could advise me on how to get law enforcement involved in an incident in the sovereign Disney World.

Insurance company's CEO

The investigators from my insurance who contacted me were so rude and argumentative that there was no way that I would even talk with them. They were allegedly in a city sixty miles from my house. I get my vehicle insurance from an agent ninety miles away in the opposite direction. There was no local representative of my insurance company. For all of my professional life, my wife took care of all insurance matters. She died eleven years ago and I just kept all of her arrangements. We never had a claim on anything, our properties, or vehicles. So now it was very strange to encounter "my" insurance company as my foe in a claim. They refused to accept a word that I told them yet they accepted as absolute truth a video that was absurd in content as dribble.

I sent a registered letter to the CEO of my insurance company and a new investigator, one in Florida, was assigned to make contact with me, but the rude, obnoxious investigator sixty miles to the west was still calling the shots. It was obvious at this point that my insurance company was now compliant with the criminals who fabricated a video to defraud the insurance company, me, and the rental car company. Not only do I have to find a way to get law enforcement involved, but I have to deal with a client-hostile insurance company.

Don-got-me lawyer

I was shocked to get a letter from a "Don-got-me" lawyer in Florida that was claiming that the bus driver got injured when he rear-ended me. I spent at least a half hour with him at the incident and he was as healthy in body as one can be. He left the scene to deliver tourists to Disney. Also, I was in the car when I got hit and there was no impact. I was angled to the flow of traffic and all that I felt was the rear of the car moving to my right. I was pushed sideways. The bus stopped with the same stopping force that occurs in a stop for a red light or stop sign. There was no crash. I am certain that the bus driver was watching a screen on his phone in the stop and go traffic that existed on One World Drive. He looked up and saw the cars (me) in his lane and stopped too late.

My letter to the Don-got-me lawyer included this description and I told him that he was participating in a felonious act since false claims in an accident is against Florida State law. I did not receive a reply. Orlando is rife with Don-got-me lawyers based on what I see on TV. They advertise several times an hour on all of the channels that I get at my *pied a terre* and a significant percentage (maybe 60%) of all highway billboards in the Orlando area advertise from $500,000 to 10 million dollars for faked accident injuries. All ads show healthy people. You do not have to be injured, just willing to lie. The Don-got-me lawyers do the rest.

I have no idea how Don-got-me lawyers can live in their skin. How can they sleep knowing that they are stealing from everybody who buys any kind of insurance and they are stifling America's entrepreneurs? Nobody with any assets can invent anything. The Don-got-me lawyers will find a way to sue you. Your business will fail because you did not put a sticker on your golf ball that goes twice as far as conventional golf balls saying "do not let your pet eat these balls"; and some dachshund ate one and died and now you are being sued for 100 million dollars or whatever the value of all of your possessions. There are apparently no limits on awards in America's legal system.

Maps of the incident

When the bus driver was moving his bus around at the incident scene, I was sketching the location in my pocket calendar. It happened at a large intersection. One World Drive is a conventional two-lanes-in-each direction expressway. The lanes were separated by a grass median that varied from about twenty feet wide to about one hundred feet wide. What was unique about where the incident occurred is that One World Drive was intersected by a road that was about one hundred feet in width with no lane markers. I entered One World Drive from a detour on the intersecting road. It dead-ended in a Disney parking lot after crossing all four lanes of One World Drive. The Disney parking lot entrance was gated and the gates were closed and the lot, which covered many acres, was empty at the time of the incident.

Google Earth can produce a satellite view of most roads on the planet. I asked my son to get maps for me on Google Earth showing all of the details of the incident site. I used their maps in my analysis of the bus company's fraudulent video. I could measure distance on the video by using an unusual Disney road sign as a distance reference. It was a sign with Mickey Mouse ears. It was unlike all other roadside signs. Overall, satellite maps of One World Drive were essential elements in my evidence of accident fraud on the part of the bus company.

Attempts to get a lawyer

The only TV that I watch is the local and national evening news. During this single hour of TV, I estimated that I get an average of six advertisements from lawyers stating that you will get rich if you have any kind of accident and have them represent you. Of course, I decided I should get millions for getting rear-ended by a bus, so I called the most prominent TV advertiser in Florida, Bombastic and Bombastic, and I got a twenty-minute question session on the phone from a sweet-talking woman who kept saying that she was so sorry about my accident, we sympathize with you. The interview ended with her asking me the details of my injuries. I said I was not injured. She asked a few more questions and then said that she was sorry but we cannot help you. She suggested contacting the state bar association for legal help.

I tried two lawyers up north. One advertises as the largest auto accident attorney in the state. His phone number is all five's. They only do vehicle accidents. This time the interview was by robot and the outcome was the same: contact the state bar association. The third lawyer that I tried was the one on the billboard across from the diner where I eat lunch on Mondays. She claims on the billboard to get results without a single digit phone number. She had a person give me the phone interview, but also said to go to the bar association when I said that I was not hurt. I believe that all Don-got-me lawyers use an artificial intelligence-based question and answer computer program that ranks responses with regard to possible money awards from a lawsuit. Of course, if you are not injured you cannot ask for millions for your pain and suffering. Suing the bus company who rear-ended me to pay for fixing my rental company car will not pay the big money that they need to pay for the TV ads.

Getting police involved

I struck out trying to get the police involved the day after the incident. My local police department in Florida could not even let me talk with a uniformed officer because the incident did not happen in their jurisdiction. So, I sent a letter to the head of the Florida Highway Patrol. I got his name from Google and my rational in writing to him is that there is a Florida State law against fraudulent accident claims and I was the victim of one. I received a letter back saying that I could discuss this with a sergeant xxxxx and they supplied a phone number. I called the number several time, but only got "leave a message" and I never got a call back.

I also wrote to the Florida attorney general, but did not receive a reply. Of course, I wrote to the governor of Florida first. I did get a reply, but it was something like: "thank you for your letter, we will take your letter into consideration in future legislation" or something like that.

Help from family

My oldest son works as a materials engineer working for a governmental accident investigation entity. They occasionally get involved with vehicle accidents and I asked him if they had an expert that they use for analyzing accident videos. He gave me the name of one and I contacted him about analyzing the bus service dash-cam video. I sent him the video by email and he wrote back his observations of the video content, but said that he could not find anything wrong with the video. He did not see any fraud. I asked him how he analyzed it and he said that he viewed it several times. It was only 23 seconds long.

I asked him if he could break it down into individual images and he said he could. He did this and emailed me 672 individual images that he said comprised the 23 second video. He did not analyze the individual images, but his general comments showed that the vehicle in most of the video frames was not mine. I went on to analyze the 672 individual images by redrawing each image as seen from above using a Disney sign as a directional marker. I found many incontrovertible evidences of fraud and I made a PowerPoint presentation (for a jury) pointing out the fabricated parts of the video. Of course, I included the fact that the video sent to the insurance company was not from a dash-cam device, but was a video of a video. A monitor was clearly shown in every image. The video was made from a monitor used to edit the dash-cam video. I sent my analysis showing the fraudulent aspects of the video to the CEO of the insurance company, but received no reply.

Video analysis

I firmly believe that the insurance company investigator that I had been dealing with from my insurance company had no idea that a video or movie is made up of individual images. Movie cameras do not leave the lenses open to make a movie. It would come out as a blur. A shutter is opened and closed to take individual images, about sixteen per second, and when they are played back, they appear as a continuous event to the human eye (really the human brain). Digital cameras also do this, but the shutter may be electronic rather than mechanical. My son's video expert gave me thirty images per second for analysis.

When I was working at Eastman Kodak, I used to do solid particle abrasion studies using high speed cameras that took 5000 frames (images) per second. The camera would shred the last ten feet of a 5000-foot roll.

Thus, videos, like movies, are made up of individual images and the only way to determine if a video is unaltered is to look at individual images and see if they are sequential or not. We used to have a film studio in my northern city that did film editing and knew about individual images. I called them and they now do only sound recording or some other thing, no movies, no videos.

Then I called my local engineering school which offers a degree in movie making and gaming. I asked them if they could analyze my accident video. They said they could, but I had to fill out a research proposal form and submit it on-line. I did so, but never heard from them.

A computer expert from my philosophy school told me that there is on-line software that is free and can be down-loaded from the internet and can be used to alter/edit/Photoshop videos. But he declined to help me in my video analysis.

Summary

My initial incident investigation did not produce much in the way of success. I naively thought that my insurance company would believe my account of the incident and be my advocate against the other person's insurance company and that they would negotiate a settlement. As it turned out my insurance company never listened to my description of the incident, only the other person's. The dishonest driver and Bus Company knowingly submitted a fraudulent video showing my rear-ending to be a side swipe. It was incumbent on me to disprove his fraudulent video, because my insurance company lacked the intellect/expertise to analyze an alleged accident video. The ten or so people that I showed it to all agreed that it was a video of a video and certainly not something suitable for evidence in a court of law. The reason why my insurance company investigators accepted an obviously "tampered-with" video is that they get paid for closing out investigations. They do not care if their employer has to pay. Their performance is probably rated on how many claims they close out. There is no concern about fraud or the effect on their company's customers.

Chapter 4
The 3-Month Investigation Trip

On September 1, fourteen weeks after my rear-ending, I made a trip from New York State to Orlando to revisit sites and try to talk with the bus company about their dashcam set-up. Why was it on at the time; where was the camera; who manufactured the equipment; how do they deal with nearly twenty bus trips a day etc? I also intended on making contact with the collision expert who examined my damage, establish what law enforcement entity has jurisdiction over the crash site and try and contact Disney security and a lawyer in Sanford. This was the purpose of the trip as well as to check on the livability of my Florida house. I had a plugged sewer on New Year's Day (2022) and I ended up getting my entire sewer lines replaced with a pumping system that I never heard of before. Does it work?

The objective of the trip was to gather facts to help in my fight to keep my insurance company from accepting the fraudulent accident video submitted to them by the bus service. Of course, the ultimate goal of the trip was to find something that my insurance company would accept. They had not believed anything that I told them to date.

My investigation started with the local police department, then the sheriff, then the State Attorney, then another sheriff's department and finally the Florida Highway Patrol. Then there was a life altering email, more law enforcement contact, then a lawyer contact, then I met the collision expert and the trip ended with an expressway toll booth audit.

Local law enforcement

According to the collision expert that assessed my rental car damage, submitting false information on an accident is a felony in the State of Florida. Of course, I expected that some law enforcement entity would be responsible for charging a person and some Florida city, town or state entity would prosecute the crime. I consulted a Florida lawyer and he agreed that the statute exists and showed it to me in a law book.

As stated in a prior chapter, the day after the incident I tried to contact my local police department. I went to police headquarters and there were two women (not in uniform) behind a glass wall. I said that I wanted to discuss a vehicle incident with a police officer. They asked where it occurred. When I told them it happened at Disney World, they immediately said that it was not their jurisdiction and they would not call an officer. This time I did not tell them where the incident occurred. I just said I wanted to talk in person with a police officer. She said she would have to call one in, they were all out on road patrol. My Florida house is in a city of 30,000 about fifty miles from Disney World. She grudgingly called an officer out on patrol; I later learned that a police sergeant was sitting no more than twenty feet from her behind closed doors.

In any case, I stood in a freezing hallway for one hour and ten minutes; finally a uniformed person with "citizen contact" or some such term painted on his vest arrived. He did not carry a gun. He went through the jurisdiction routine. I argued: "what do you do if a person is a victim of an internet crime like the ones where people are conned into sending gift cards to a post office box. He did not answer. I insisted on filing a crime report. He said, "let me talk to my supervisor" (the sergeant behind closed doors). He came back and insisted that they will only deal with crimes committed within the city limits. He had no answer about internet crimes. I knew that getting useful help from my local police was a long shot, but since I pay their salary (my property taxes) I wanted to see if I could get a return on my money. The answer was "no".

In an effort to get something of use out of my trip to police headquarters I went back to one of the girls behind the glass and asked her who prosecutes crimes. She said the State Attorney. I thought they might have a district attorney. I guess not. So, I asked if I could talk with a state attorney. She said that they are located on the city's main road four miles away. She made me a Map Quest to show their location. I drove there directly from police headquarters. It turned out to be the county court house.

There were two uniformed sheriff officers standing by the court house entrance. I told them I was trying to report a crime associated with an incident at Disney World. They both said that I would need to go to the Orange County Sheriff Office. They had jurisdiction over Disney World. They gave me their address. They said that they are from another county so they could not deal with anything associated with Disney World.

I said I still wanted to talk with a prosecutor. They pointed the way to the State Attorney office. I had to go through a TSA-like security to get into the building. The State Attorney office was on the second floor. There was only a receptionist there. I told her my plight and she said that the State Attorney at her office only does her county's State Attorney stuff and besides there were none there. I gave her my argument about there being a state law with nobody willing to enforce it or prosecute it. I said that this is like the Texas school massacre incident. Twenty people lost their lives because one hundred law enforcement officers called did not have the jurisdiction to go in after the shooter. She said that that's the way it is. I left and went home. I would try the police with the "jurisdiction" in the morning.

This day, I started my wild goose chase with phone calls. I started by calling the Orange County Sheriff's Office. They told me that they do not go to Disney World and its property for traffic accidents. They said the only exception may be if their jaws of life equipment or something like that is needed. They said that you want to contact the Florida Highway Patrol. I told them that I already wrote to the head of the Florida Highway Patrol (FHP) and I received a letter to contact officer xxxx.

I did a number of times and it is one of those "leave a message and don't bother me" numbers. "I'll not call you back".

However, undaunted, I called the FHP number that I got from the Orange County Sherriff's office. I got a live person on the phone who said that they do not deal with prosecuting false accident reports to insurance companies. These would be prosecuted by the State of Florida's Financial Services Division. He did not tell me who they were. He said that I would need a lawyer. I sensed that it was the familiar brush-off. Who am I to ask a law enforcement officer to enforce a law?

I agree whole-heartedly with the FHP person. I need a lawyer. I tried to get one on my last data-collection trip to Florida. I did get one to talk with me in person (for $320/hour). I also got him to send an email to my insurance company. It was written in legalize and I do not know what it said. He told me that it said: if you settle the claim for more than my insurance limit ($300,000) we will sue you. My insurance company contact did not like this letter. She said: henceforth all communication will have to go through his law firm. I copied him in on her email and somehow, he got her to continue talking with me.

In any case, I tried to once again talk with the lawyer. I emailed him for a meeting. He sent an electronic meeting form back. I did not know how to use this system, but I thought that I booked a meeting at 12 noon tomorrow. I showed up at noon at his office and he was not there. I talked with his secretary/aide and gave her a USB drive containing the fraudulent video, a PowerPoint with my accident account and a PowerPoint of my analysis of the fraudulent video. My hope was that he would look at all these and decide to represent me in my efforts to do something about the fraudulent video.

The new video email

I do not have access to the internet when I am at my *pied a terre* in Florida. I occasionally check my email at the nearby public library. I also use their computers to check into my airline flights and get boarding passes. When I checked my email on day two of my investigation trip, I was surprised by an email from my insurance company. She said that the bus company submitted the original video. It was obvious that the video that I received from the insurance company was a video of another monitor screen. I mentioned this many times to the insurance company, but they insisted that the video was reviewed thoroughly by their investigators and it is valid and well-made and accurate.

Needless to say, I was shocked that the insurance company would accept a new video that was altered to eliminate an obvious flaw in their scheme. I told the insurance company contact that I cannot view it on the public library computer that I was using. I checked on it, but it did not play. I am not sure if I could even try to look at it. I know that it is fraudulent; I know what happened. I was there. What was on the video never happened and I am still in disbelief that my insurance company will not accept anything that I say as true. They taped my first phone call and maybe they detected anger or something in it. In any case, I gave the insurance company no other response than, "I cannot open it on my Florida trip."

Bus company visit

The most significant thing that I wanted to accomplish on this investigation trip is to see the dashcam installation, to get details on make and model, its location in the bus, its capture equipment and their procedure for using it. Is one on at all times?

I expressed these questions to my insurance company contact and she sent me an email telling me to contact Abdullah at this phone number. I also wanted to visit the bus company to get a feeling for them as a legitimate company. I Googled them the day after the incident and an address was posted on International Drive, near Orlando resorts.

I Googled the bus company to check the address before I drove to International Drive and Google said that the bus service did not have a physical address. You deal with them online. With no option to drop in on them, I called the phone number that I got from my insurance company and asked for Abdullah. Much to my surprise, Abdullah answered the call. I introduced myself as Ralph Swartz (one of by book pseudonyms) and I said I was hired to analyze their accident video. Abdullah said that he would not answer any questions about their dashcam system. I asked if I could see the bus installation and their office. He said that if I show up at their office I would be asked to leave. I asked where the office was and he hung up on me.

And that was the end of my attempt to get details from the bus company on how they use dashcams in their business. Not to be deterred, I drove around Orlando looking for a Best Buy. I found one and asked if they sold dashcams. They directed me to the dashcam aisle. They displayed fourteen different brands each doing something different from the others. They even had models that output to cellphone apps. Of course, once something is a video on a cellphone you can do anything that you want with it. America's Funniest Videos TV show did a bit where people faces were changed into animal faces. There is no limit to how one can alter a video. I Googled editing videos and countless u-tube videos showed up on on my screen. I cannot believe that any insurance company would accept a home video as a legal document, but that is what my insurance company did.

Toll booth audit

On my way back north, I acquired information on toll booths on the expressway that I took to Disney World on the day of the incident. This whole mess started because One World Drive, the road to Disney World, was barricaded when I was a few miles down it. There were no detour signs and I ended up driving aimlessly through Disney campgrounds and the like and ending up back on One World Drive when it was open again and plugged with the 100,000 cars a day that show up at the Magic Kingdom.

I left my house which is fifty-nine miles from One World Drive at 7:00 AM. I estimated that I arrived at 8:15 and found the road barricaded. I also estimated that my detour took fifteen minutes and that put me attempting to get on One World Drive at about 8:30. The bus company video showed that it was made at 8:09 AM on May 15. If I could show that I was elsewhere, like on the expressway, at that time it would completely void the fraudulent video.

I told this to the insurance company and they asked for my toll receipts for the expressway. I did not save them. The tolls near Disney were only $1.00 or $1.50 and I did not ask for a receipt. However, I paid these tolls in cash and the expressway had a separate lane every five to ten miles where you get out of the travel lanes and stop to pay a live person your toll in cash. This is where you can also get a receipt. This time I got receipts and I asked one toll booth attendant if they photograph license plates at the toll booth. She said they did. I asked if I could get a copy of their surveillance video and she gave me a brochure on how to contact the expressway authority.

If I can get a surveillance video showing my car at a toll booth at 8:09 AM it will automatically void the fraudulent video. I think. In any case, I planned to contact the expressway authority. I have been using this expressway for several years and in 95% of my stops at their toll booths I was the only car. There are two lanes on the main expressway for vehicles having an Easy-Pass license-recognition system. Hardly anybody, but me, pays cash. The rental car had a transponder system, but I did not know how to use it. Thus, it should not be an awesome task to review an hour's worth of license plates to find mine. It may only be sixty cars, one per minute. I decided to pursue this as part of my seemingly hopeless effort to show the truth.

CEO letter

Since I really did not have any clear-my-name successes on this trip, I decided to end it with a letter to the CEO of my insurance company. I made up a list of facts (twenty items) regarding the accident claims to go with the letter. I also planned to send the fraudulent video, my what- really-happened PowerPoint and the PowerPoint that I have been working on to refute the fraudulent video. In the letter I asked the CEO how I should proceed.

I have no way to ensure that the CEO will get my letter, much less look at the stuff that I sent, but I am in a hopeless situation. I have already lost my personal life to this crime. What else do I have to lose?

Trip summary

In a word, this investigation trip was another failure in my attempt to fight a crime. The felons are winning. Abdullah may have been the master-mind of the fraud. He may have been on the other end of the bus driver's phone as he moved the bus around the blocked highway.

However, the most demoralizing result of the trip was the email sent to me by my insurance company containing another fabricated video that I needed to analyze. I was there; I know what happened. As a follow-up I would try to get surveillance videos from the expressway authority, but there were no other positive results.

Chapter 5
Thrown Under the Bus

On September 28, I received an email from my insurance company with an attached demand letter from the law firm representing the bus driver. They wanted $300,000 by October 20. I do not know what a demand letter is, but I was told by an ex-police officer that it is from a court and it is a big deal. I forwarded it to the lawyer in Florida that I have been trying to get to work with me on reporting this fraud to law enforcement.

Concurrently with the demand email I got an email from the claims manager of my insurance company saying that my insurance company is blaming me for the incident and that both videos submitted by the bus company were authentic and unaltered even though one was 23 seconds long and the other was 90 seconds long and they were different in everything, but this weird image intended to make it look like my Honda darted in front of the bus. The bus driver apparently took it when he was moving the bus around after rear ending me. I suspect that Abdullah was directing him.

It is the purpose of this chapter to chronicle the immediate actions that I took after learning that I was thrown under the bus by my insurance company. The objective of the chapter is to show the world how Don-got-me lawyers get the enormous amounts of money for faked injuries.

The first action on my part was to try and get legal assistance; then I tried to get the second video analyzed; then I tried hiring private investigators; then I decided to step back and review all of my law enforcement actions and try anew to find somebody who will listen to a victim of accident fraud. That will be in a separate chapter. The chapter will summarize my treatment by my auto insurance purveyor.

The scam police

A week before my thrown under the bus event, I attended an old-person group luncheon where the luncheon speakers were two retired police officers. They had an entertaining routine to warn old people about the many scams that criminals target old people with. They went over "the grandchild was arrested and needs bail money" scam and the one where "you won the lottery and need to pay the taxes up front" scam and many others. They worked for an elder advocacy organization.

I did not have time to talk with the scam experts after their talk, but I saved one of their brochures and called one of them several days later. The scam expert told me that getting a demand letter was a big deal and I needed to get a lawyer. I told him how I had been turned down by every lawyer that I talked with, about ten lawyers. As soon as I say I was not hurt they refer me to the state bar association. They will not talk with me.

The scam expert gave me a list of phone numbers to call for possible help. I had hoped to hire one of the scam experts to help me get law enforcement involved. He did not seem interested. Everybody that listens to my tale of woe has a phone number for me to call.

Help from Disney

I mentioned in Chapter 3 that I tried to contact the general manager of Disney World for closing times on their highway into the Magic Kingdom and if I could get a statement from the security person who witnessed the bus driver's antics. I gave them his name and employee number. I did not get a reply in two months from the general manger of Disney World so I sent a "Full Monty" letter (overnight, certified, to be signed for) to the CEO of the Disney Corporation. I finally got an email from an executive facilitator or some such thing, saying that she contacted me to placate the boss. However, a week later I got another email saying they may help with the road closing, but they were getting hit with hurricane Ian and could not do anything right now. Weeks went by without a response for my request for help from Disney on incident details. In early November, I sent a registered certified overnight (a $32 Full Monty letter) to the CEO of Disney Corporation. Then I got another response (around November 20) from the Disney World customer service person saying that they will not let me contact the Disney security witness to my incident without having a subpoena from the court. She also said that she contacted their Reedy Creek Partners, whoever they are, and they said that there were no road closures on One World Drive on May 18, 2022 even though I encountered a full barricade across both inbound lanes.

On November 20, the Wall Street Journal reported that the Disney CEO that I had sent three Full-Monty letters to had been fired by the board of directors. The company brought back the person who was previously CEO and officially retired several years earlier.

Thus, it was now quite clear that the root cause of my accident, Disney's barricaded road, is denied by Disney (they lied) and they reaffirmed that they will not help anyone hurt by Disney on their property. As a corporation they have complete and absolute contempt for their customers. In my case, their customer was the conference that I was attending that had 1300 delegates, most staying at one of their resort hotels.

I do not know if their CEO got fired over his customer-contempt attitude, but it certainly in my opinion should be a reason for firing a CEO. The costumes and smiling masks of Disney "cast members" may be hiding angry hateful people who also have nothing, but contempt for Disney park visitors.

I sat next to a Disney "Snow White" once on a flight from Orlando to New York. We talked the whole trip and I concluded that she was a happy, talented person (a college degree in voice) and was essentially enslaved by Disney World. She was paid hourly (she did not say how much), but she typically worked sixty hours a week; did not own a car and lived in a Disney compound for cast that cost most of her paycheck. She liked people. I know that all Disney employees do not have customer contempt, but I know with certainty that Disney policy makers have contempt for customers. Besides this incident, as I mentioned previously, I tried to leave the Magic Kingdom during the daily parade and learned that all park exits were closed. I was held against my will. Both times I went to the customer service office near the exit and was told "too bad. This is what we do. If you don't like it then go to the Splendid China theme park in Kissimmee.

The Disney monopoly allows this kind of behavior. They get up to 250,000 people a day coming to the Magic Kingdom, and they could care less if some are dissatisfied with their visit.

Help from private investigators

I tried to find people on the internet and any other place that could help me show to my insurance company and Florida law enforcement that a significant criminal element is running loose at Disney World.

I read in a story in a Florida newspaper about a private investigator who was giving a talk on elder fraud in a nearby town. I wrote to him to try and hire him to investigate the bus company. I got no reply. Next, I found a private investigator on Google maps within a block of the bus company's location. I contacted them and received the same no-response that I got from the private investigator in the newspaper.

My conclusion is that these companies do not want to get involved in vehicle incidents. Maybe they subsist on tracking cheating husbands.

Why did my insurance company do this to me?

It is very hard to conceive of any business of any type treating customers as adversaries. How can such a business model be sustained? There are no words to adequately describe my treatment by my insurance company. Why did they treat me as the adversary and the person who hit my stopped vehicle is treated as a fully believable injured party? I notified my insurance company the day of the incident by phone and they assigned me a claim number. I told them that I was rear-ended by a bus. The bus drove away without exchanging the information required by Florida law. It was a hit and run and two weeks later I was notified by my insurance company that I sideswiped the bus and was being sued by the bus driver and that the insurance company accepted the fabricated dashcam video as incontrovertible evidence that I had sideswiped a bus and caused serious injuries to the driver. This was the situation on June 6 after a May 18 incident.

When I reported the incident to my insurance company, I fully expected them to handle it. To me it was quite straight forward. I was stopped in stop and go traffic, thousands of vehicles heading to a

9:00 AM opening of the Disney's Magic Kingdom. I was struck from behind by a bus where the driver was on his cellphone. This is why the bus continued to push my vehicle sideways well after contact. His sight and attention were on his cellphone. One of the videos submitted by Bus Company showed his phone sitting flat on a ledge to the left of the steering wheel. I suspect that viewing stuff on his cellphone was part of his daily work. He had a boring job. Shuttling tourists to Disney, hotel to Disney, every day all day. He could be in another place and another situation on his phone, a fantasy world. I believe that cellphone distraction was the root cause of him rear-ending me and that he worked for a company that was just a money maker for the bus company owner, the mayor of a city in the Philippines. He only expects a continual flow of money from the bus company staff to him. He is not concerned with operational details like honesty.

There was a similar situation that made the news in my city of residence. A non-citizen operated an escort service as a side source of revenue. He hired a driving staff and spent no money servicing his vehicles. One vehicle carrying seventeen people speeded down a hill and crashed into a shopping center at the base of the hill. The brakes failed on the vehicle. All the people in the vehicle were killed – including a bachelor getting married the next day, the driver and one person in the shopping plaza. The escort business was not the real business for the owner, just a money-making sideline and a court decided that he did not maintain his fleet of vehicles.

I suspect that this is the situation with the bus service that owned the bus that rear-ended me. It was not a real business with an owner or shareholders. It was a side venture by a wealthy Philippine politician. This is why the bus company faked an accident video. I suspect that they may have the dashcam video as part of their business model. If there was a way to check, I suspect that accident scams with their fleet of buses was a revenue stream for the company.

What is certain about the bus company is that they would not allow me to see their facility, their dashcam recording policy, their protection from alteration of recorded videos, where the cameras are in buses and how often they record and what do they do with daily recordings. I physically tried to visit the bus company at the address on the web site. I called the bus company person who gave the video to my insurance company. He only gave the name "Abdullah" to the insurance company. I called about a visit to the company. Abdullah told me not to come. If I show up, I would be escorted out.

How the insurance company "investigator" became enamored with the bus company is beyond my comprehension. After my second call I established the following image and sent a letter to the CEO asking for something better. Without a doubt he had insufficient intellect and social skills to hold any job dealing with other people. He was rude and argumentative to the point of being obnoxious.

When I wrote a letter to the insurance company CEO about his rudeness, I got a reply that a woman in Florida would be my new contact with the insurance company. She was less belligerent, but neither she nor any other person at the insurance company listened to a word that I said on the phone or wrote in emails. I never had in-person contact with a person even though the vehicle incident involved a loss of $300,000 to a fraudulent claim. About a week after the incident the insurance company investigator got an alleged dashcam video from the bus company and this sealed the investigation and all discussions with me. I was convicted of sideswiping even though the video that was sent by the bus company to my insurance company was incontrovertibly not unaltered output of a dashcam. It was a video of a computer monitor. I showed the submitted video to at least a dozen people not concerned with the incident and they all agree that it was a video of a computer screen, not device output. Most dashcams output to an SD card.

I had now spent more than 600 hours of my time analyzing the two videos sent by the bus company and trying to get the insurance company to listen to me as well as trying to get law enforcement involved.

My perception of my insurance company is that the company exists as a company only on paper. There is a corporate headquarters that rents a floor in an impressive office building in New York City. They have accident offices in each state with several people associated with that "office" but the "office" is just a mail box at a UPS store and all state employees work from home. Every person that I encountered in my, now six-month, ordeal works from home. Most of my phone calls had dogs barking in the background. The arrogant, argumentative, rude and obnoxious person that was assigned to my claim was likely working out of his house in his pajamas. The only hint of professionalism that I got in all of my contacts was the person who took my claim over the phone. She was civil and professional. I also had trust in the CEO because there was feigned response to all three of my letters to him. He tried to get some effort from his staff in response to a customer concern. He failed, but at least he tried.

In summary, my insurance company came across to me as a paper organization, with no physical location for most employees. They mostly work from home and have no comprehension of accident videos and no interest in learning about them. The investigation employees get paid the same if they win or lose a case so they take the easy route and throw people under the bus to end a claim so that they can get back to tending their dog and watching soap operas. This is my impression of my insurance company even though they are one of the ten largest in the USA with more than 30,000 employees. Where are these people? I have no idea. They certainly do not interface with their customers. They certainly are not customer advocates.

Conclusions

1. Your insurance company can be your adversary in an accident.
2. An insurance company can have no competency in analyzing dashcam videos.
3. There are no resources to the average person to analyze an accident video for fraud.
4. Law enforcement will not provide any help in the legal resolution of an accident.
5. There is no way for an average automobile owner to vet an insurance company for competency.
6. There is no way to talk in-person with an auto-insurance company employee.
7. All decisions of accident fault are made by unknown entities within an insurance company. There are no judge and jury. You have no say.
8. Some insurance companies totally ignore candidate social skills in hiring staff.
9. Customer satisfaction is not part of the mission statement of auto-insurance companies.

62

Chapter 6
The Disney Dilemma

The incident that this book is about happened on Disney property and was directly caused by Disney World's road barricading. I was probably one half of a mile from making it to my 8:30 meeting at Disney's Dolphin hotel when I encountered a physical barricade across the two expressway lanes that lead to the hotel. The only way out was to take the side road at the barricade. This side road meandered all over Disney property and dumped me into a maelstrom of traffic near the entrance and parking lot for Disney's Magic Kingdom.

It is the purpose of this chapter to chronicle my attempts to get the Disney World leadership to allow me to get a statement from a Disney security person who was a witness to my "incident" and to find out the exact times of the road barricade to deal with the bus driver's fraudulent video. The objective of this chapter is to make the Disney Corporation aware of the consequences of their disregard for the people who attend events on Disney property and people who visit Disney "Resorts". They are not happy places when it comes to public safety and consideration of customers.

The chapter format is to discuss my historical association and safety issues, then the barricade experience, then my efforts to make contact with live people within the organization, then deducing the incident location in the park.

Historical association

I think that my first trip to Disneyland was in 1966. I was involved with friction and wear for my job as a materials engineer and at that time most of the conferences on these subjects were held on the west coast. I would fly into Los Angeles once a year or so and usually I would try to stop at Disneyland on a free day before or after my conferences. I took my wife the first time that I visited Disneyland and we went on rides and did all of the tourist things. Thereafter, I would go for the day and people watch and eat at some of their novel restaurants. A visit to Disneyland without rides was $10.00 for all day. It was pleasant just taking in the sights and sounds. I had been on all of the rides so there was no point of repeating them.

One time when my three sons were teenagers, I was attending a conference in LA and my wife called me and said that she had to go to the hospital and have an operation for a burst appendix. She said that she was sending the boys to me. I can take some vacation time and show them Disneyland. She arranged for them to fly out and I met them at the LA airport. It was the first Disneyland visit for all three sons. They loved it. I did the rides with them. Everything was a wonderful experience. Interestingly, I was attending a meeting during the 2021 pandemic at a hotel that abuts Disneyland. I tried to visit the park on a free afternoon and I was not allowed in. They told me at the gate that you have to apply for tickets on-line and they have daily quotas that are full for the next six months.

I do not know when Disney World opened, but my wife and I bought a rental house in Orlando in 1983. We would make an annual trip to Orlando to inspect the rental house and talk with our rental agent. This annual visit always included a visit to one or more of the Disney attractions. We usually went to Disney's Magic Kingdom. In fact, that is when I first encountered Disney's barricaded road and barricaded park exits. My wife and I were exhausted. We had been at the Magic Kingdom since 9 AM. It was now 4 or 5 PM. The afternoon parade was about to start and we wanted to go back to our hotel on nearby International Drive. We fought our way through sidewalk crowd's five people or more deep. Sometimes we could make progress towards the exit by walking through connected gift shops and snack shops. When we finally got to the exits, we found them barricaded. We could not get out of the Magic Kingdom. We were being held against our will.

The reason for the barricaded exit was allegedly the parade must enter on a street that runs parallel to the exit turnstiles. We had to wait an hour or so for the parade vehicles to pass our location until we could cross the street and make our way to the exits. When we got out, I went to customer service to complain. They essentially told me: "tough", this is what we do and we do not care that you wanted to leave before the parade."

This same thing happened another time when we were with my mother-in-law. She got sick and wanted to leave before the parade. The exits again were barricaded. We had to wait to the end of the parade. This time I wrote to the park manager. The results were the same: We do what we want to do and public safety is not something that we are concerned about.

I had the rental property in Orlando for 32 years so we had 32 years of visiting Disney parks. I also ran into road barricades on coming into the Magic Kingdom. We waited since there was no other alternative. We asked at customer service and we were told the road was barricaded without notice and without detour signs when the parade vehicles need to process to the park.

In investigating my 2022 incident I learned from a Disney cast member that the only road in or out of the Magic Kingdom is barricaded every night when the park has fireworks. The barricade starts about one half hour before the fireworks and lasts through the fireworks. I do not know the reason for this barricade because the fireworks have always been over a lake, not over One World Drive. Maybe Disney does not want people viewing the fireworks free by parking on the entrance road.

In any case, the cavalier closing of the only road in and out of the Magic Kingdom whenever Disney management wants to do so creates what may be the worst public safety risk on the planet. Before the pandemic about 500,000 tourists would fly and drive into the Orlando area to visit the area's theme parks each week. On an average day, the Magic Kingdom may host 200,000 visitors. If there is some kind of emergency like a fire or explosion during an exit barricade there could be a tremendous loss of life.

Almost every year, the media reports on a garment factory fire with closed exits killing hundreds, or a theater that catches fire with locked exits and hundreds perish. What could happen at a Disney Park would kill tens of thousands of people – many children.

Disney security and the incident

About five minutes after I was rear-ended by the tourist bus, a Disney security person came down the exit from the Magic Kingdom side of One World Drive and stopped where the bus was blocking both inbound lanes to the Magic Kingdom. Police or emergency vehicles could not get past the bus. He was backing up traffic back to the interstate miles away. This Disney security person had me move my car from the angled position where I was rear ended. I parked in the left inbound lane. Now traffic could flow if the security person could get the bus driver to move his bus from blocking both lanes.

The bus driver was on his cell phone continuously and was moving the bus all over. I had no idea what was going on. I now know that he was following the directions of the person who was to make the fraudulent video. He took video clips at the rear ending; then he backed up maybe ten feet.

Then he backed up maybe fifty feet – this is when he blocked both lanes. The Disney security person tried to get the bus driver off his phone to no avail. He moved the bus around all sorts of angles for about thirty minutes. The Disney security person went to his vehicle and came back with a State of Florida accident form that is required of all vehicle accidents. It contains name, insurance and vehicle information of both vehicles. He gave me a copy on his personal clipboard and I filled out my portion and he tried to get the bus driver off his phone to fill out his portion. I filled out his license number portion. I went around the bus and looked for an owner's name. I found one written very small on the side and I wrote down the license number. Then I cornered the bus driver and tried to get him to fill out his name and insurance company. He scribbled something on the document that was not legible and said he had to go and drove the bus away.

I was left with my car blocking a lane and I was still talking with the Disney security person. He gave me directions on how to get to the Dolphin Hotel. It was back several miles on the exit side of One World Drive. He was extremely helpful. I had no idea where I was on Disney property. When I turned at the One World Drive barricade onto the only intersecting road, I essentially ended up on Disney's back lot maze of buildings and parking lots. There were no people visible in any direction - just buildings, roads and parking lots – no street signs, no directions. It was beyond frightening.

Getting a witness from Disney

When I got to my conference hotel, I noticed that I still had the Disney security person's clipboard with the state accident form on it. The clipboard also contained the daily car inspection sheet that the security person filled out. This gave me his name and employee number. I called the Disney World 800 number and asked for security the day after the incident. I could not get past the ticket sellers. Besides trying to talk with the incident witness I wanted to prove that One World Drive was barricaded when I tried to get to the conference hotel. Somebody ordered the barricade. Somebody did the barricading. Somebody knows the time that the barricade went up and went down.

The time-stamp on the bus video was 8:09 AM to 8:10 AM. If I could show that the road was closed at that time it would show that the video was fabricated. In one of my phone calls to Disney World, I got the cast member on the phone to admit that they close the road any day that they have fireworks. The time of the fireworks varies throughout the season with sundown and they close one-half hour before the fireworks and keep the road closed for forty-five minutes. Hundreds of thousands of Disney customers would be trapped in the park in the event of some emergency like a bombing or shooting or fire.

After phone contact with anybody in authority failed, I wrote a letter to the General Manager of Disney World. I googled the "head of Disney World" and I got a woman's name and an address of Buena Vista Drive. I saw that road sign in my trips to my conference hotel so I know that the road exists, but my letter was returned (after one month) with a note on it: addressee not at this address.

Then I wrote to the CEO of the Disney Corporation, Robert Chepak. About two weeks later I got an email from an executive assistant saying that they got my request and will look into the matter. On September 28, 2022 I received another email saying they are investigating, but they have a hurricane to deal with. Hurricane Ian crossed Florida that day. Also, that day I received notice that my insurance company threw me under the bus and declared that I was at fault for the sideswipe that never happened.

No maps

When I was rear-ended, I had absolutely no idea where I was. When I encountered the barricaded road to the conference hotel, I turned right on the only road available. I had no idea where it went. It went to the incident.

I was so preoccupied by my being lost that I asked the bus driver where I was. He told me by the Magic Kingdom entrance. When the Disney security person showed up, I asked him if I could get a map that shows where I am and how to get out of there and get to my conference hotel. He replied that there are no maps of Disney World or the Magic Kingdom.

I have no idea why the Disney Corporation bans maps of their attractions but it certainly is not helpful to customers to not know where they are. Google Maps and GPS on phones and devices can be used to find specific Disney attractions, but I am a map person, I want to know where I am with respect to everything at all times.

I drew the intersection where I was rear-ended in my pocket calendar. I showed all of the features and estimated distance. I was so shocked by my rear-ending that I did not think about photographing the situation with the camera in my briefcase. I never brought it out. However, the most important photo would be when the bus was in contact with my rear driver's side tire. I could not have gotten the actual contact photo because the bus driver backed away about ten feet before I had a chance to open my driver's side door and get out.

I had no idea that he was a crook working for a crooked company at that point. This situation started to show when I could not get the bus driver to fill out the accident report given to us by the Disney security person.

Deducing the Disney property

As soon as I got back to my office in New York I emailed my son and asked him to give me a Google Earth view of Disney World. He knows how to do this kind of thing and I do not. He sent me an email with a Google Earth image of the Magic Kingdom.

No wonder I was completely lost when I encountered the World Drive barricade. Google maps showed that the only way I could drive on from the barricade took me through an incredible maze of buildings, roads, alleys, highways through jungles, warehouses, roads etc. I only remember one sign "Disney Wilderness Resort". There was a perpendicular road in the jungle area with this sign. It may have been Disney's campground for people who drove RV's.

It seemed like I was on this road for hours. At all times I scanned in all directions for a person, an office, any sign of life. I found none. No people for what seemed to be an eternity. The Google Earth satellite image of the area confirmed what I saw as I drove. It was like a thousand-acre attic. I finally narrowed down the intersection of the incident. I took a transparency and copied the roads and grass areas from the computer monitor with a marker pen. It matched the sketches that I made in my pocket calendar at the scene. The intersection was huge and very strange in configuration. The road that I was on was intersecting but not at a right angle, maybe 75 degrees and it crossed all six lanes of One World Drive and ended at a chain link fence. It looked like the fence was an exit from the 500 or so acre Disney parking lot that was in use, but there were no cars in the area of the incident. It may have been an overflow lot. I did all of my video analysis based upon distance and location offhand from Google Earth images. I could zoom in and out to identify landmarks.

What was incredulous in the second video was that it showed "my Honda" coming from some fly-over road. I remember seeing it on Google Earth, but I had no idea where it came from. So, I was connected by a fraudulent video showing me coming from some fly-over road that I would have no idea how to get onto the road. It took me two days to find One World Drive to get to my conference hotel.

By this time, I was convicted by my insurance company, so there was no sense in finding out where the fly-over road came from. The bus driver knew the area intimately since his daily job was delivering tourists down One World Drive. He likely knew every bump on the road.

Disney the Adversary

After I was thrown under the bus by my insurance company (October 6), I got a call from the boss of the insurance company claims manager that I had been dealing with. The claims manager's boss made the call and he had another person on the line that was the head of some other department. Apparently, these two insurance company executives were in possession of the video and two PowerPoints that I sent to the insurance company CEO a week or so earlier.

Of course, they questioned all of my statements on the PowerPoints and everything I said. I really do not know why they called, because they did not believe anything that I said. They asked lots of questions, I gave them truthful answers, but it was very clear that they were only calling because of my letter to the CEO. They never listened to a word that I said.

I made it quite clear that the insurance company neglected to contact the only incident witness, a Disney security person. I gave them his name and employee number and asked why they did not contact him or find out about the time of the One World Drive barricade. One of the men on the phone said that they had previous dealings with accidents on Disney property and that they as an organization are uncooperative. He said that you need a subpoena to get them to supply needed accident information. They know that nobody can touch them and they do not care about any accidents and the like among vehicles on their property unless it involved damage to their property.

The Florida lawyer that I talked with (at $320/hour) told me that if you shoplifted something in a Disney store the Orange County sheriff would be there in ten minutes to arrest the person, but they will not come for an accident unless a jaws-of-life is needed to extricate accident victims.

Because of Disney World's status as a sovereign nation within the USA they can do anything that they want and this is what they want: taxpayer-paid-for theft protection at no cost and they do not want to know about any vehicle accidents that do not damage Disney property. This is my interpretation of what the Florida lawyer told me. Disney is ruthless and without ethics. They have evil as a core attribute (along with greed), my opinion.

Disney Engineering

One time I attended a technical society meeting where the events keynote speaker was the Disney World's chief engineer. He had a staff of more than one hundred engineers and their responsibility was to design the mechanisms for the robotic characters that are everyplace throughout the park. The demands on these machines are significant. Most robots move continuously when the park and attractions are open. Often the robotic character is synced with words or music. Some have to go underwater; some have to do things on demand, like when a boat approaches a campsite of native people.

The usual engineering steps must be followed to make rides and animated characters: the process starts with a concept, then a preliminary design, then a design review, then design implementation, then debugged, then redesign, then production tests etc. It is a rigorous process.

This same level of detail has gone into the physical layout of the Disney complex. They have to have a bevy of civil engineers to layout the roadways and parking lots that bring customers to the park. The intersection where our "incident" occurred is about as complex as any intersection can be and it had no traffic controls. There were no stop signs or stop lights. Thus, Disney World seems to ignore traffic control. Once roadways are designed and built, they are probably turned over to a "grounds crew" or some such organization and they may not have the authority to install traffic controls.

The incredible engineering failure of the Disney Corporation at Disney World is their wanton disregard for people using their roadways. I got into a traffic maelstrom because I ran into a barricade on One World Drive with no detour information. What are cars and service vehicles supposed to do when the grounds crew decides to close the entrance and exit roads? Apparently, they do this at will with complete and absolute disregard for the users of those roads; their customers and suppliers.

Disney Public Relations

On September 27, more than two months after my first letter to Disney Management about the Disney security person, I got a letter from a person from "Executive correspondence" about my request to get road closure information and a statement from the Disney security person who witnessed my "incident". The letter stated that I would have to sue the corporation or get some legal entity to get a statement from their incident security person eye witness.

They said that they would continue to try to get the information that I requested on road closures. Months have gone by since this last email. It appears that Disney Corporation's official stance is: We are ignoring your request for a statement from our security guard witness of a vehicle accident and injury on our property.

Fixing Disney

Theme parks have a viable and noble purpose, but what can be done to solve the tragedies like mine that they cause. I suspect that the root cause of Disney's contempt for customers comes from their bigness and monopoly status. It is a monopoly because I have personally witnessed its competitors die. My personal favorite theme park, Splendid China, died in the 1990's; Sea World lost its sea creatures to the animal lovers, (who usually have a dog enslaved for life); Cypress Gardens lost its water skiers and so on. There are still a few other theme parks in the world, but most have a fraction of the patronage of the Disney parks. Disney is an entity not unlike a US government agency. They are all impregnable to citizens. For example, I have tried everything imaginable to get law enforcement at any level involved in this crime to no avail.

Maybe some Disney executive will have the foresight to consider their theme parks' susceptibility to terrorists and psychotic people attacks. Mass murders are now common around the world. Almost daily some terrorist group commits a horrendous act. At Disney World in Orlando no police will venture on Disney's forty square miles without some clandestine arrangement. For example, police would not come to my incident, but I am told they respond to Disney's request to arrest somebody shoplifting at a Disney store.

After mass murders became common in the USA Disney instituted a check of bags and the like that people bring into the park, but people are gathering in huge groups as the tram from the Disney parking delivers people in hundreds to the entrance area. A psychotic or terrorist could have their weapon in their car or truck. Or a vehicle could be loaded with explosives or worse. People could die and be killed in a stampede. I recently remember standing in a huge crowd of thousands, shoulder to shoulder, waiting to get on a boat to go across a lake to get into Disney World. Even a cherry-bomb going off could produce a stampede, like the one that recently occurred at an Indonesian soccer game killing 125 people. Queues of thousands of people can lead to this type of disaster especially with little ones in the queue. Queues of hundreds and thousands are unnecessary. Disney has an engineering staff. A methods engineer could eliminate the incredibly dangerous queues that I encountered at Disney World in 2019.

However, the easiest disasters to prevent are the ones posed by closing park exits during parades and closing roads in and out to attractions with no forewarning. I ran into a barricaded road with no forewarning and no detour information or any information at all on what to do.

Unannounced Disney road and exit closures are nothing but wanton disregard for human life.

There is no excuse for this; there is no way to keep such reckless actions from causing more harm if a psychotic or terrorist event should occur. It is tantamount to allowing a suicidal passenger with a bomb on an airplane with six hundred passengers (yes, six hundred, I flew once from Toronto to San Paulo that packed.).

Corporate greed may be behind Disney's wanton disregard for public safety.

If my plea for public safety never makes it to Disney's executive row, wherever that is, then maybe the State of Florida's initiative to reign in Disney World in Florida will produce positive results. As I write this, nothing has transpired to change the Disney dilemma. I was told that implementation of the directive that ends Disney World's status as a sovereign nation within the USA does not start until 2023.

I do not know what the transition to control by elected officials will involve, but it is rumored that Disney will have to pay for public police and first responders. They will have to start paying property taxes like American citizens and there will have to be some sort of government for the sovereign entity connected to a Florida "country" under USA's state and federal constitutions. I certainly hope that the conversion leads to a reversal of Disney's wanton disregard for the safety of the people who visit their attractions worldwide.

The Disney Hotel Problem

Many national and international organizations hold conferences in Orlando because Disney World and other theme parks often prompt conference attendees to bring their families and visit the Orlando attractions and there are enough hotel rooms for even huge conferences. I have attended many technical conferences in Orlando hotels and in the Convention Center. The conference that occurred during my incident catastrophe was held in a Disney hotel within the Disney World Resort. It was a truly inappropriate venue. The hotel had nice meeting rooms, but they were scattered over acres of hallways and steps and foyers. It was almost impossible to go from one paper to another since it may involve a five-or ten-minute walk. The papers were only twenty minutes long plus ten minutes for questions and there was no walking time allowance between rooms.

However, the most egregious problem with a Disney Resort venue is unforgiving isolation from everything. It was like being dumped on a desert island. There were no restaurants for lunch; there were no attractions to visit; there were no shops except Disney trinket shops. From the practical standpoint they were dangerous in the event of any kind of situation that requires civilization. There is no police protection, no ambulance service, no way to deal with a medical or any other type of emergency. Staying at the Disney World Resort is like an ocean voyage in a ship that had no backup plan for storms, or ship propulsion failure. The hotel that my conference was held in did not even have phone access. If a person called the hotel looking for you, they would be greeted by a robot that tells the caller to use the internet to perform whatever service you want, like a reservation.

Unfortunately, technical societies and other organizations that have conferences do not seem to be aware of the incredible safety risks that arise from on-resort venues. I have another conference to attend in a month in a similar venue. These organizations often select hotel venues based upon lowest cost room rates to attendees. There is a reason why theme park hotel room rates are low. They are inappropriate places to have an event that involves meetings and mingling of attendees. Orlando has every sort of hotel, shop, and restaurant outside of theme parks. Theme parks are inappropriate places for any kind of conference, meeting or convention. They impose personal risk to such a degree that they should never be considered. I lost my life and all of my possessions to attending a conference at Disney World in Orlando. And the Disney organization is absolutely responsible, but because they have the status of a sovereign nation there is no legal recourse.

I suspect that organizations that book theme park hotels as conference venues will become liable for disasters like mine. I hope that this message somehow reaches them and they opt for venues outside of walled theme parks. This is my opinion based upon 40 years of personal experiences. Theme parks are not suitable venues for technical conferences.

Summary

I now consider Disney World in Orlando the most dangerous place on the planet. When you go there you lose the rights and protections that you expect as an American citizen. I went to attend a technical conference and ended up losing everything. Disney was the cause and Disney refused to help.

I became the victim of a Disney-based vehicle accident scam. My Google searches of Disney incidents suggest that it is a minefield of other scams particularly if you are from a foreign country. There are similar scams, for example, for shop lifting at a Disney store, arrested people pay large sums of money just to go back to their countries. There is no advocate for customers. Terrible things can happen and you cannot do anything about it. The two times I tried to leave the Magic Kingdom during a parade and closure examples I was not permitted to leave the park. My family and I were held against our will and nobody in customer service or the Florida police cared. I was told: "This is what we do" If it caused damage to you, too bad. You cannot sue them because no lawyer will take the job (I tried). You cannot complain to elected officials. There are none in the sovereign nation of Disney World. You cannot call the police; they do not venture into the Disney "nation".

What can be done about the Disney Dilemma? The most effective option is usually legal action. Lawyers know how to hurt people and entities of all sorts. I point-blank asked a Florida lawyer if he would take on a 100-billion-dollar lawsuit against Disney World on my behalf. He said, "I am an honest lawyer. I could take your money, but nothing would happen. You will never get any law enforcement agency to help and your insurance company abandoned you. There is nothing that I or any other lawyer can do. It would be like trying to sue the President of the United States".

Petitioning the CEO or Disney Corporation is sort of in the same category. I sent a letter to the CEO and after a month or so I got an email from a public relations person at Disney World saying they would not allow their Disney security witness to talk with me or an outside entity. There is an impenetrable iron wall around company management.

How about a social media condemnation of Disney? I read an article in the Wall Street Journal in 2022 about the daughter of Walt Disney producing a documentary condemning Disney Corporation for their current misdeeds. I was not able to get a copy of this documentary, but I suspect that it was not substantial enough to change anything in the way that Disney Corporation operates. What may work in this area is a TikTok video showing Goofy scamming an old person. Too bad I do not know how to make TikTok videos.

I guess that all that I have available to get justice from Disney Corporation is prayers. We Americans successfully used this weapon against the USSR during the Cold War of the 1960's. The USSR collapsed during the Reagan administration. We prayed for the conversion of Russia. We did not get a conversion, but for about twenty years their leaders started to behave like a civilized nation. That ended in 2022 with the Russian invasion of the Ukraine and war crimes against all who occupied lands that they decided to take.

How about enforcing ethics and morality into Disney Corporation? Does a giant corporation have a conscience? Does a corporation have behavior traits? I spent thirty-eight years of my work life with a giant corporation that dissolved into the ether after 110 years of existence. They lost their ethics; they lost their morals; they went astray in attitude. They lost their focus on making a product that people want to buy. They turned their focus to creating societal change rather than a product.

My internet studies of Disney suggest that they may be heading on the way to being "Kodaked". Google suggests that the "Magic" is fading in the kingdom. Walt Disney had a vision of a theme park where families could come and have their children enthralled by characters and rides. Parents would be pleased with the safe, orderly operation of the Disney attractions. Both are fading. Maybe somebody in Disney's leadership will have sufficient insight to suggest a return to ethics, morality and family fun.

I will pray for that to happen. That appears to be all that I can do to address the Disney Dilemma.

Chapter 7
The Law Enforcement Dilemma

Law enforcement in the USA is discretionary. A uniformed officer can decide to ticket or not; a prosecutor can decide to prosecute or not; some laws were enacted for political purposes and legislators did not care if they were enforced or not. In addition, all government employees and elected officials can use the "jurisdiction weapon" to do nothing about a request for a government agency to perform the function in their title. As an example of the latter, at the time of this writing, an abortion decision is being decided that affects all of the USA. A district court in Texas made the initial judgment, but other courts are claiming to be higher than the US Supreme Court which declined the case. Apparently, there is no way to rein in the "jurisdiction weapon". It can be used for anything that the government does or does not do and citizens of the USA have no say in the matter. Jurisdiction comes from a higher power that is not made known to citizenry. My latest attempt to get law enforcement involved in my problem was a letter to the head of the FBI.

My incident certainly was a federal matter. It was over the $125,000 criteria for federal involvement (I was sued for $300,000). It was more than a one-state incident. I am a New York resident and the incident happened in Florida. It also had international ramifications since the bus company that made the fraudulent accident video was owned by a mayor of a city in the Philippines. It may be that the fraudulent video scam is being used by entities all over America and it is part of an international assault on the USA.

In any case, the FBI sent me a form letter saying that they sent my incident report and request for investigation to offices in Florida and New York.

I was sent down to "jurisdiction" black hole

And this is how any government elected official, appointed judge, government service or government agency can opt out of performing their designated function. The founders of the USA's constitution obviously needed to define "jurisdiction", and put in some controls on its use to not do your designated job.

The purpose of this chapter is to review my attempts to get law enforcement help at each level and to illustrate what should have happened at these levels. The chapter objective is a behavior modification on the part of government officials and uniformed officers. We injured could use some 'Samaritan" empathy. The chapter starts at the crash scene, then city police, then county police, then state police, then requests for help at the federal level.

Crash scene

I suspect that all uniformed police officers who drive about all day in patrol vehicles do not want to spend their day responding to fender-bender accidents. Thus, they opt not to respond unless the 911 agent tells them that somebody is trapped or that people are hurt where they need on-site medical treatment. Even if there is a need to extract victims from a crushed shape, they can still use the jurisdiction weapon. In my town, only town police show up for car crashes; so if you have a crash in a part of the USA where jurisdiction may not be firmly established you may be left to die.

Jurisdiction trumps all matters

I did everything wrong in dealing with my rear-ending. First, I allowed the bus driver to call for the local police. He told me that he called and they were not coming. I do not know if he called anybody. He was on his cell phone for every second that he was at the scene. He may have been talking with the person who was directing him on production of the fraudulent video. He may have called his wife. I should have called 911 myself.

The crime that was committed at the crash scene, fabrication of a fraudulent video, would have not been possible if a police officer was there. The bus driver moved the bus around at least ten times, blocking tourists to Disney World for about one-half hour. Any law enforcement officer would not allow this. Of course, I had no idea what he was doing. I never thought in my wildest dreams that the bus driver was busily formulating an accident fraud to cover his running into a stopped vehicle. I am certain that he was watching something on his phone that laid on the dashboard of the bus.

Because of the traffic snarl caused by the fraudulent video antics, a Disney security officer showed up at the scene, but because he did not have a badge or gun, the bus driver paid no attention to him and continued to move the bus around. Since I had no idea what the bus driver was doing, I talked with the security person about getting out of the traffic mess and about how to report the rear-ending. He was courteous and tried valiantly to do something about the bus blocking everything, but the driver repeatedly ignored all of his requests.

What should have happened is that the Disney security person should have been allowed to call in uniformed law officers (with guns). A security person without the means to establish security is absurd. The bus driver was 6'2" and about 220 pounds. The Disney security officer (and myself) was 160 pounds and 5'9". This is another reason why the Disney security person was ignored.

If a uniformed law enforcement officer (with a gun) does not show up to a crash scene, you are susceptible to accident fraud and any other type of crime or behavior that a vehicle crash can produce.

No cop, no hope of establishing fault

County Law Enforcement

Where I live, there must be a secret jurisdiction agreement between the county and state uniformed officers. It has been my observation that the town police ticket speeders on town and county highways in the town and the state police ticket speeders on the interstate feeders that run through the town. The sheriff (county police) seems to only use his uniformed officers and vehicles to move prisoners around. The sheriff is the only entity that can incarcerate people. The towns that make up my county do not have their own jails.

Thus, if you are involved in a vehicle crash on an interstate you may get help from the state police, but it appears that county police (sheriffs) are "jurisdiction outed" from vehicle crashes. I called all of the sheriff's offices near my Disney crash scene and they all "jurisdiction outed". I ran into some sheriff deputies outside of a courthouse near Disney and they in unison jurisdiction outed. In fact, they made me feel like a significant intrusion into their courthouse gathering. I walked away with no help whatsoever in trying to get law enforcement involved.

Naively, I contacted the county sheriff's 100-million-dollar forensic services facility in my home city to see if they would help investigate the fraudulent video that the bus driver sent to my insurance company. The head of the fifty-person - 100- million- dollar facility told me that they were jurisdiction outed. No matter that I pay their salary with my property taxes on five properties in the county. They only use their fifty-person, 100-million-dollar facility on issues that they deem to fulfill their jurisdiction requirements.

You would think that these people would welcome a job to examine a video for authenticity since they are supposed to use science to solve crimes like on

TV. I have never heard or read any media reports on crimes that they solved since the facility was built for 100 million taxpayer dollars five years ago. They must enjoy boredom.

State Police

One would think that state police would have jurisdiction over accidents and crimes (like fraudulent videos) that happen outside of cities, towns or counties. I guess not, I did receive a letter from a State Police Office, after a letter to the Governor of Florida, but he jurisdiction outed. He sent me a letter to call a person in the state police that was never at the phone designated in the letter. After multiple calls to this number, it was quite clear that that person had also jurisdiction outed.

It would certainly be helpful to US citizens if they were apprised of the jurisdictions of the various levels of uniformed and non-uniformed officers that we taxpayers fund. What are their responsibilities? What determines jurisdiction? Every crime, every accident in the USA occurs under these three levels of law enforcement. Who do we taxpayers petition when we want to report a crime or vehicle crash and are jurisdiction outed by each?

State Laws

Florida State Statute 87.234 (Title XLVI, Chapter 617) clearly states what happened to me, accident fraud is a felony crime. However, no law enforcement agency is listed in the law as having the responsibility of enforcing this law. I wrote to the governor of Florida several times and got handed down responses from state police leaders. It was clear that the governor never saw my plea for enforcement of Florida Law 87.234. Every now and then a law enforcement officer would drop me a nugget of information that might be helpful in solving the crime that was committed: fraudulent accident information. One uniformed officer out of the hundreds that I petitioned for help, suggested that I go to the Florida Office of Financial Services to seek enforcement of Florida Statute 87,234. I was unsuccessful in many attempts to find the Florida State Government entity entitled "Financial Services".

After no measureable success at the town, county, state and governor levels, I took the desperate route of going to law school myself. I bought a sixty-four lecture (1/2 hour each) DVD course on "Law School for Everyone". The course was eye opening. There were four professors from famous US law schools who presented the lectures and I learned many things pertaining to my case.

The most significant thing I learned was that lawyers are absolutely not interested in their client's culpability. In accidents, there is absolutely no concern if a client is incontrovertibly lying about an accident or injury.

A lawyer's only concern in any legal matter is winning.

All four of the world-famous professors in my DVD course regarded Johnny Cochran, the lawyer who absolutely annihilated the prosecutors in the O.J. Simpson murder trial with theatrics involving a pair of gloves. Every professor showed that overpowering government prosecutors is the goal of criminal law and submission of juries is the goal in civil matters.

The basis of all law enforcement in the United States is adversarial. Prosecutors must argue better than defendants in criminal matters and lawyers for the plaintiffs have to out-argue before a jury and the lawyers for the defendants. It is their game. It is no different than my high school debating society. Interscholastic debating was a big "sport" in my high school. It was right behind football and boxing. Each debating team was assigned either the pro or the con on an issue and those who argued best won. This was so even though the cause being argued may be "Why the USA should use nuclear war on the Soviet Union". One team would have to argue that the USA should kill millions of people. There is no concern about the ethics of nuclear war. I guess that is why I never tried out for the debate team. I could not force myself to argue for something that is morally wrong. Morally wrong means people set up rules of behavior in their conscious brain that they try to live by. These rules of behavior (morality) are all that separates human beings (homo sapiens at present) from animals. Most animals eat each other. There are no behavior rules in the non-conscious autonomous portion of the brain.

It was really quite eye-opening to me that ethics, morality, religion, beliefs, etc. are not part of the lawyer profession. How sad. Lawyers appear to be taught to win at any cost. It does not matter that you are arguing the end of humanity. I have no idea how lawyers reconcile this issue in their own consciousness, the part of the brain controlled by the individual.

However, the thing that I learned pertaining to my quest for justice for the crime committed against me is that prosecutors determine everything with regard to law enforcement. To get enforcement of Florida Statute 87.234, I would need to find a prosecutor who would bring a case against the bus driver who submitted the fraudulent video. No uniformed police officer would submit the paperwork necessary to prosecute the bus driver. No county prosecutor would prosecute the bus driver because the accident occurred at Disney, even though the crime (fraudulent video) occurred in cyberspace. The video and all correspondence were on-line. It was not in any physical part of the USA. Still, I was not able to get any government prosecutors interested in enforcing Florida Statute 87.234 or any government forensic lab in the United States interested in scanning the two fraudulent videos that the bus driver used to convict me and steal $60,000 from a benign insurance company.

Federal Law Enforcement

I was really disappointed with the response from the FBI. They jurisdiction-outed. If any crime needed federal intervention, it was the crime done to me. It happened in a designated no-law enforcement part of the USA. It affects USA's worldwide status since Disney World in Florida is the most popular travel destination in the world. Visitors from all countries are subjected to no-law enforcement when they visit that attraction. The internet is rife with accounts of scams and frauds carried out on foreign visitors in the sovereign nation that is Disney World. As an aside, the government of Florida tried unsuccessfully in 2023 to reign-in the rogue nation that is Disney World. Before the Florida legislators could enforce their attempt to bring law and order to Disney World, Disney countered by establishing laws that will allow them thirty more years of "Disney Law" instead of law and order by the standards imposed on all other US businesses.

Disney World is more powerful than the State of Florida and the FBI.

Summary

What is a crime victim to do about no law enforcement help? I petition anyone who will listen. My only hope for justice is for all nine justices on the US Supreme Court to read a copy of this book which I will send to them at my cost. Hopefully, my "arguments" for enforcement of Florida Statute 87.234 show that what was done to me was unconstitutional (no due process) and they will submit a court order to the State of Florida demanding enforcement of Florida Statute 87.234. Hopefully the Supreme Court will mandate the assignment of a federal prosecutor to prosecute the bus driver who violated Florida Statute 87.234 and the use of the State of Florida and the FBI forensic labs to examine the fraudulent videos for authenticity.

When the bus driver is found guilty of violating Florida Statute 87.234, the assigned prosecutor shall then prosecute the bus company that produced the fraudulent videos as a co-conspirator. This is my law enforcement expectation.

The law enforcement dilemma is that in the USA laws can be created with no way for the law to be enforced. Enforcement of laws is up to the discretion of prosecutors most of whom are not elected or known to the US citizenry. They can prosecute or not, based upon their personal opinions and all law enforcement in the USA is ultimately controlled by jurisdiction mandates that may be unknown to most citizens and may be totally incommensurate with the wishes of American citizenry. Americans certainly have no say in any law enforcement jurisdiction issue and that is part of the dilemma.

Chapter 8

The Insurance Company Dilemma

Introduction

My auto insurance company ignored my constitutional right to due process. I was convicted of causing an accident and I lost my life because my insurance company refused to listen to my accident evidence. How do auto insurance companies operate and why would they execute a customer who gave them money every month for decades without receiving anything from them other than monthly bills?

This question is explored in this chapter. It is also the purpose of this chapter to discuss how auto insurance companies react to an accident; how they reacted to my accident and in general how auto insurance companies operate.

The chapter objective is to alert readers of the perils of reporting an accident, the treatment of policy holders after an accident, and what people should consider in shopping for an auto insurance purveyor.

The chapter starts with my interpretation of how they operate. Then we discuss auto insurance from the consumer standpoint. How to decipher an insurance policy is discussed. Then we enumerate the details of making a claim. The chapter ends with a list of things to do after an auto collision including how to deal with your insurance company.

How Auto Insurance Companies Operate

There is insurance available for just about anything. The concept of insurance is to get lots of people to agree to give the insurance company a regular sum of money, an hourly, daily, monthly or yearly premium, in return for the insurance company paying for some catastrophe's cost if such a cost occurs. The insurance company has to take in more than it pays out for catastrophic events to make a profit. There is risk on their part of having catastrophic events cost more than they take in in premiums; so to survive, they need to accurately predict claim payments and premium income. They take data on many things to keep an imbalance from happening.

I recently read about an insurance company who offered to pay elderly people for nursing home care if needed. A couple bought a policy at retirement that cost about $3000 a year. After four years, the premiums had increased to about $13,000 a year. This company did not assess the future nursing home cost situation accurately.

Insurance is a gamble on the part of company and client. Gambling casinos have to keep the slots and tables paying out no more than 90% of gross revenues. They live on the 10%.

Auto insurance companies have a "leg up" on other insurance companies in that most states in the USA mandate that every vehicle on their roads be insured for some minimum amount of insurance. Most states also have a mandate that vehicle owners have insurance for uninsured vehicles. Even with laws to make auto insurance mandatory, a significant percentage of vehicles on US highways (maybe 13%) do not have any insurance. If you are involved in a collision with an uninsured vehicle your insurance company may pay damages of you have the necessary "coverage."

There are three major types of coverage in most automobile insurance policies:

liability

collision

comprehensive

Liability covers the cost of a collision if you cause the collision. It pays for damages to the vehicle that you hit as well as for medical expenses for those that may have been injured by you colliding with another vehicle or stationary object. This part of a policy will have limits like "30/60/30" which means the limits of dollars in thousands that will be paid out for different accident situations. The first number (30) is the most that will be paid by your insurance company if one person is hurt. The second number is the most that the insurance company would pay in a single accident regardless of the number of injured people. The third number is the most that the insurance company will pay out for property damage, regardless of how much the actual cost is.

Most states have a minimum for these three liability values. You can buy more and increase these accident maximum payouts for higher premium costs.

When a person claims to be injured in an accident and hires a lawyer, the first thing that the lawyer does is to establish the insurance limits on the policy of the person accused of causing the accident. If your coverage is like the 30/60/30 state minimum the lawyer may not take the case. Lawyers get one third or more of settlements and he or she may not want to be troubled for only one third of $30,000. In my case, my middle number was $300,000 so that is what the Don-got-me lawyer requested of my insurance company.

Lawyers know that it will be difficult to get money from an individual like me who has little to none. They know how to easily get money from insurance companies: piece of cake.

Getting back to the types of insurance, collision is the insurance that you can buy to pay for damage to your vehicle from collision with another vehicle or object. Most states in the USA do not require motorists in their state to have this coverage. Also, most policies have a deductible, like $500, so they will not pay for the first $500 of repair costs. If you make the deductible higher, the premium usually is lower.

The third type of insurance offered by most auto insurance companies is comprehensive. This covers things like vandalism and glass breakage that is not caused by a collision. Comprehensive may or may not have a deductible like collision. If a stone from another car breaks your windshield comprehensive may cover the cost of replacement.

In summary, insurance companies take in premiums from many individuals and pay claims for incidents to only a few individuals each year. To stay solvent, they have to pay out less than they take in. About 250 million vehicles in the USA have auto insurance. The average monthly premium is about $150. About 30 million vehicles on the road carry no insurance. The industry as a whole is worth about 330 billion per year compared to 100 billion per year for all American automobile manufacturing. My auto insurer had more than 30,000 employees in 2022 and made more than twenty billion dollars in profit.

How does one buy auto insurance?

The simple answer is through an agent. An agent is an insurance sales person. Their job is to sell policies with monthly payments. They get a monetary award for initiating a policy and may or may not get "royalties" from continuing policies. Insurance agencies often sell policies from other companies. Sometimes they are sales people for only one company. Agents advertise to get new clients. Their role can be that of an advisor on what policy limits to buy and what "add- on's" to elect. They are insurance consultants.

When I built a new house, I had to shop for an agent to sell me a policy. You do not buy policies direct from the insurance company for the kinds of insurance that most ordinary people buy. Some kinds of insurance are so expensive that it is, for practical purposes, unavailable to ordinary people. When I wrote my first book, a college textbook on engineering materials, I was concerned that I could be sued for something that I wrote, like titanium 6Al/4V does not corrode in 4 molar sodium hydroxide and somebody tried this couple and it corroded. I could get sued. In any case, I did not get liability insurance because the annual cost would be ten times my annual royalties. I have been "winging it" since 1979.

What I know about selecting an automobile insurance agent is: nothing. When I started driving at age sixteen, my parents took care of my car insurance. I bought my cars and paid for all repairs and the like, but I have no idea what transpired with regard to cost and who the agent and company were. I was probably on my parents' policy or something.

I had two accidents in my first four years of driving. I fell asleep at the wheel the day after my junior prom. I had not slept for about thirty-five hours and I passed out in an instant on my way home from my girlfriend's house. I almost made it home. I climbed a telephone pole about 1000 feet away from my garage. My father paid to fix my car. There was no insurance company involvement. The telephone poles, (there were actually two banded together), were not damaged.

My second accident was a rear-ender. I was in bumper-to-bumper, stop and go traffic and the car behind me started tooting his horn. I looked in my rear-view mirror for an instant and the car in front of me stopped. I messed up the bumper and hood on my beloved 1952 Mercury convertible. I hit a 1947 Hudson that weighed 8000 pounds and resembled a Sherman tank. There was no damage to his car and I fixed mine. The tooting behind was a friend who noticed that I was in front of him. Thank you. I fixed my car myself. I taught myself auto body repair and I used that skill for another forty years on subsequent cars.

I got married about two weeks after graduating from engineering undergraduate school. From then on, my wife handled all insurance and financial matters. She was really good when it came to insurance matters. Somehow, she became good friends with a person in an insurance agency that sold all kinds of insurance. This woman became our penultimate adviser in auto and other insurance matters. She remains in that position today, but to a lesser extent because my wife has been dead for eleven years at this writing.

The insurance that I had at the time of the Disney collision scam is whatever my wife negotiated during her fifty years of caring for all of our household matters.

In summary, you get auto insurance from an agent and it helps to have a spouse who investigates all options and selects what is best for your household. I have never had an insurance claim so I do not know anything about how insurance companies work or what agents do. The Disney accident scam has made me a researcher in such matters.

Deciphering a Policy

In my attempt to hire a lawyer to fight the Disney accident scam, I managed to pry forty-five minutes of counseling from a Florida accident lawyer. He told me that auto insurance policies contain wording that essentially says that they, the insurance company, can opt to do whatever they want with regard to deciding who was at fault in a collision. If they think that their costs will be lower in paying a claim, rather than fighting a claim, they can say an accident was your fault even though you have incontrovertible evidence that it was the other person's fault.

I got a copy of my policy and it did not contain any such verbiage. It was one page with my policy payout limits and countless other pages on non-related things like accident prevention and discounts for safety features on my auto. It contained no information on how they determine who is to blame. I was rear ended while stopped. Period. I recited this to them at every opportunity.

To somewhat resolve the matter, the accident attorney that I was fortunate to get any help from, wrote a letter to my insurance company stating that if their payment for the Disney accident fraud exceeded my liability allowance of $300,000 that we would sue the insurance company for the overage. This was my only legal help in the whole sordid affair.

He had to do this because if the insurance company accepted a claim of ten million dollars from the fraud people, I would be personally liable for ten million minus $300,000. According to the Don-got-me ads of the lawyers in my city, they typically get car accident judgements of one to ten million dollars even if you have no measurable injuries, only pain and suffering. Pain and suffering as well as anxiety, depression and trauma are not measurable or quantifiable. This is why Don-got-me lawyers never have a personal injury without them. Pain is worth $50 per day times the expected life of the injured. Anxiety is worth $30 per day times the expected life and so on. I suffered traumatic stress disorder caused by the rear ending by the Disney accident scam bus. If I could identify a lawyer to represent me, I would sue Disney for my "injury" and to me it is worth $10,000 per day until death. Since I have already lived past the expected average life of a USA male of 76 years, I would not be able to use the $30/day claim for trauma for life since my life is technically over.

I find it absolutely preposterous that the bus driver that rear ended me claims back injury. My insurance company sent me an email showing that the bus driver has a severe lower back injury that was shown by an MRI and may require surgery.

My insurance company had their serious-injury staff call me; I think that their names were Larry and Moe. They said that they were assigned to my claim because back surgery was needed.

Nobody from my insurance company ever questioned the bus driver's medical report. I was never shown any medical report and of course, I know that the only injury suffered by the bus driver was loss of his immortal soul. Obviously, he is not concerned about his soul. He lied to everybody he could about what he did to me.

He was looking at his phone in stop and go traffic. I was stopped in his lane when an important message came on his phone. He pushed my car sideways about a foot. There was no impact and he tore a piece of rubber off my car when he backed off after hitting me.

A standard part of engineering is calculating force on moving machine elements. I calculated the sideways and long axis force that the bus would see if I sideswiped the bus as the bus company claims. The longitudinal component of a sideswipe by a 2900-pound Honda HCV at an acceleration taken from individual images from the bus company video was twenty-three pounds. The longitudinal force was 123 pounds. How could either of these forces injure a bus driver in a 40,000-pound bus traveling at 30 mph? The sideways force would not move the bus sideways any more that a wind gust. The same is true with the longitudinal force. It would only add more propulsion to the bus's motion down the road.

Of course, there was no person in my insurance company even remotely interested in analyzing the bus company fraud. The contact person in my insurance company told me to send my investigation evidence to some mailbox in a remote area of New York. I sent PowerPoints and evidence against the Disney accident scam to the insurance company's CEO (in a certified, overnight mailer costing $32 each time). Larry and Moe responded to one CEO letter. The others only garnered a terse email from the assigned company contact at some undisclosed location in Florida.

One time I begged my Florida contact person to meet in person with somebody from the insurance company. I said that I would travel wherever necessary. I know that they had an address in New York City and Google said that they had offices in Hartford Connecticut and St Paul, Minnesota. The insurance company responded by saying that they forwarded my query to two people that were someplace. I never heard from either of them about an in-person meeting.

Apparently, it can be impossible to have in-person contact with an auto insurance company regarding a claim.

After six months of continual contact with my insurance company by phone and email I have the following vision of how the company functions.

There is a CEO in a sumptuous office on the eighth floor of a nice building in Manhattan. There are two dozen bosses in this location whose job it is to meet with the CEO and dispense orders downward on how the premiums and payouts are doing. The bosses in Manhattan have a skeleton staff in each state and country where they do business. They do not have offices for the supervisory staff. They work out of the homes with their animals and school age children. The state/country supervisors have adjustors, data collection and finance people to report to them. These people are younger and work at home in their pajamas. They have smaller children and barking dogs.

The only way that my insurer's employees who "work" at home know anybody else in the company is from a Zoom meeting. Zoom meetings are not regular so the only bond and relationship between employees is a paycheck with the company name on it.

I do not know if other insurance companies operate this way, but it is the best way to make a profit. My insurance company made 22 billion dollars in 2022. Google did not say how many of their customers were thrown under the bus to make such a profit happen.

Getting back to the subject of this section, what's in your insurance policy, I have no idea. My insurance agent would answer all of my questions about coverage, but she avoided any discussion of my claim like the bubonic plague.

Insurance policies can only be interpreted by the agent who sold you the policy.

Making a claim

When I was rear ended by a bus I was in such a state of shock that I never gave a thought to the things that should be done when you are in a collision with another vehicle. There is a litany of things I should have done. We will enumerate them later.

As soon as I was able to extract myself from the Disney main gate mayhem, I finally got directed to my conference hotel by Disney security. I sat distracted through the day of talks. Incredibly, I kept thinking, "I hope that the bus driver does not lose his job for rear ending me." While also thinking how incredibly dangerous it is for public transportation companies to allow their vehicle drivers to have a cell phone on their person. Study after study shows that addicted cell phone people cannot refrain from looking at the device for more than a few minutes. The average phone owner checks his or her phone four hundred times a day. Phone addicts cannot really do any job that requires one's attention. In fact, I cannot think of any job that can be done properly while a cell phone is within reach. The bus driver that rear ended me walked about talking on his phone for at least a half hour. I had no idea that he was being directed by his employer to move his bus about to achieve various dash-cam video directions on my vehicle. The fact that he could never in the half-hour take his eyes off his phone makes it certain to me that he was watching his phone when he rear ended me.

In any case, the morning after the incident I drove the rental car to the rental car pick-up at the airport and told the rental agent that I was rear ended and the rental car was damaged. She gave me a form to fill out. It was like the State of Florida form that I received from Disney security. It just listed the names of the owners of the vehicles involved and details of what happened. I also called my insurance company. The insurance form is at least six pages long; it is written in print font so small that it could only be read under a binocular microscope and you have to initial six places and sign at the end while a long line of people behind you are waiting to rent a vehicle.

Never buy insurance from a car rental company.

My insurance company assigned me a claim number and emailed me a form to fill out resembling the standard forms from the rental agency and State of Florida. Getting a claim number started the process of paying for damage to my rental car. Never did I imagine that the bus company would concoct a personal injury claim from the bus driver. He hit me. I was stopped. He did not get hurt. There was no impact or source of energy to produce injury.

The way that an auto accident claim is processed is that a person is assigned to the claim to establish who was at fault and to assess the extent of property damage and personal injury. Come to think of it, nobody from my insurance company asked if I was injured. I was assigned an adjustor/investigator. He called me and asked me what happened and said that my phone call would be recorded. I told him what happened. I was stopped at an angle while maneuvering into stop and go traffic and the rear of my car was pushed sideways while I was stopped. Giving a phone statement to a claims adjustor was my biggest claim mistake.

Never under any circumstance agree to make a statement about an accident to an insurance company over the phone.

Never having had any kind of insurance claim in my entire life, never did I realize that my insurance company was my principle adversary.

Your insurance company may be your biggest adversary.

I was so naïve that I thought that my insurance company of more than fifty years would believe me and be my advocate in getting money from the bus company to fix the rental car. Two weeks after I submitted my claim, I got a phone call from my insurance company saying that the bus company submitted a dash cam video showing that I hit the bus, not that the bus rear ended me.

The video ended all questions about blame in the eyes of the adjustor. He put everything in motion to pay the bus company. I asked to see the video and he emailed it a few weeks later and immediately I emailed him and told him that it was fraudulent. It was a product something akin to "Photoshop", a digital editing software. I went on to prove this and do all sorts of things to show the fraud. Nothing mattered. The adjustor, who was probably a millennial in his pajamas in a wooded area in upstate New York, made the irrevocable decision on receipt of the made-up video that I was at fault. I spent hundreds of hours and thousands of dollars showing how the video was concocted to no avail. The adjustor had spoken and nothing, not even the insurance company CEO, could change the imperial edict for the adjustor in his pajamas in front of a computer monitor.

Never, ever, talk with an auto insurance adjustor without the presence of a lawyer.

Who knew? My insurance company was my worst enemy. It was far more hateful and contemptuous than the people who concocted the Disney auto accident scam.

Your insurance company can be enemy number one.

The way that an auto accident claim is supposed to work is if the incident involves people, you must immediately hire a lawyer. Once you have a lawyer, he or she will direct your contacts with the insurance company. It will be their lawyer talking to your lawyer. You will get a notice of claim from the other lawyer and your lawyer will plot a course of action.

The way that the lawyer vs. lawyer negotiations work is secret, but basically the insurance lawyers will offer something to the injured party and they will barter about the settlement amount. Your lawyer is the one that must try to clear you if you believe that the other person was at fault. There will be a lawyer for each vehicle and lawyers for the insurance company. My most huge mistake was not having a lawyer.

Never make an insurance claim without a lawyer.

I did not voluntarily make the mistake. I could not get a lawyer to represent me. I called the largest Don-got-me in the USA and the largest in my home state. They both turned me down. I was turned down by every accident lawyer that I could get the phone number of. I told them than I was not injured. This one sentence stops all negotiations. They slammed down the receiver: "We are sorry that we cannot represent you, please contact the bar association in your area."

You cannot be defended by a lawyer on a vehicle collision if you do not claim to be injured. You are injured. Your injury may be feeling uncomfortable or uneasy (something unmeasurable).

What to do? You must claim injury. If you do not observe any negative physical changes, you must go the pain and suffering route. You must make your distress caused by the incident an injury. You can call it anxiety, mental anguish, worry, listlessness, trauma, a mental health issue etc., anything that cannot be measured by a medical professional with the best analytical equipment in the universe.

You are injured in any collision

There is no alternative; you will be thrown under the bus like I was if you do not claim an injury. Looking back on my incident it was the most traumatic event in my life. It has been nine months after the incident at this writing and I spend almost every waking moment of the days that I have left trying to clear my name. I am truly injured, but since I stated over the phone to an adjustor from my company that I was not injured, that sealed the issue. I cannot ever claim injury. A phone conversation without a lawyer forever established that I cannot claim an injury or that the accident was not my fault.

Summary

The insurance company dilemma is: we are forced by US government regulations to buy insurance from any vendor if we want to drive an automobile on US roads. There is no way to know if a candidate vehicle insurance vendor is competent, honest or even respectful. We pretty much have to rely on agents for counseling on insurance company selection and what to buy in the line of insurance. Insurance companies do not have to have any in-person contact with customers and agents may also never have in-person contact with insurance buyers. Auto insurance is an ethereal business. You never get to know the purveyors of insurance products or to get jargon-free clear documentation of your coverage.

Insurance is supposed to pay money for unanticipated catastrophes in return for your monthly/yearly payments. You will never find out if you made the right company and policy decisions until it is too late. You only find out what you bought when it is too late to return it. Your insurance company may be a complete loser.

This is the insurance company dilemma.

I get a sailing magazine that has a monthly boat disaster feature. It is a description of a harrowing event on the water that the boaters had to unexpectedly deal with. The feature ends with tabulations of: what we did right and what we did wrong.

Applying such a list to my incident:

What I did right:

nothing

What I did wrong:

1. Went to a conference at a Disney hotel
2. Kept the auto insurance company selected by my wife in 1965
3. Did not make a video of the bus driver's moving the bus antics
4. Did not take photos of everything at the scene.
5. Did not get the name, address and phone of the Disney security witness
6. Should have kept the Disney World inbound traffic lane blocked until some police arrived (even all day)
7. Thought that my insurance company would be my advocate

8. Thought that my insurance company could be trusted
9. Thought that a bus company would be an honest business
10. Claimed to not be injured
11. Thought that I would not be convicted without due process
12. Thought that an insurance company has a physical location with people who worked with each other, who learned their craft, and became competent
13. I could trust others
14. No lawyer
15. Talked on the phone with my insurance company
16. Believed in due process (14th amendment of the constitution)
17. I believed that I could get law enforcement involved because what the bus company and their lawyer did was a felony crime under Florida law
18. I thought that I could hire a lawyer even though I claimed no injury
19. I should have called an ambulance, left the rental car blocking the Disney entrance, called the rental car company and went to the hospital for observation and testing
20. I should have had the bus driver sign a document showing that the bus rear-ended me
21. Should have gone on the bus and got the name, address and phone of every passenger and asked each what they saw

22. I should have taken photos of all bus passengers
23. I should have photographed the entrance of the bus and the location and sighting of any dash cam
24. I should have recorded all statements from the bus driver
25. I should never have trusted the bus driver to be a normal, decent human
26. I should have called a Don-got-me lawyer at the scene.
27. I believed in human beings and institutions.

I did nothing right and everything wrong.
Hopefully this book will give some guidance to others in selecting an auto insurance company. I opted for the highest cost company and got abysmal insurance results. Also, it is my intent in writing this book that some accident lawyers may stumble on it and be converted from Don-got-me mode to honesty and that life is not about pleasure and possessions. Life should be your "thank you" to your creator.

Chapter 9
The Lawyer Dilemma
The Problem

I stopped watching TV because I can no longer tolerate the incessant ads from Don-got-me lawyers and drug companies. Governments that are concerned about the welfare of the people that they govern will forbid advertising in all media for "products" that incontrovertibly bring pain, suffering, ruined life, disability, and death to people influenced by the ads. In the USA, cigarette and liquor ads are banned, but not other known deadly substances and practices like marijuana and speeding in automobiles. Many automobile manufacturers have professional drivers recklessly drive through cityscapes to sell their vehicles as weapons to kill others. They also show how their vehicles can destroy the environment by plowing up wildlife habitat to reach the top of a hill in what is supposed to be protected forest or mountains.

TV ads work; an incontrovertible evil to mankind can be sold to a susceptible public.

This is the "Don-got-me" problem. Lawyers have convinced the general public that all "accidents" can lead to incredible wealth even if you have no medically measurable injuries. All of the ads show happy health people getting millions from insurance settlements that that they obtained. We have one Don-got-me lawyer in my home town that found a woman with a limp to do an ad, but out of ten to the seventeenth power ads that I have seen it was the only one that suggested that real injury can occur in a vehicle accident. All other ads send the message:

We can get you millions in any suit that involves an insurance company or similar guaranteed source of money like a government entity.

The purpose of this chapter is to discuss how Don-got-me lawyers operate. The objective is to show Don-got-me lawyers that what they are doing is unethical, immoral, damaging to their profession, and wrong for the continuation of civilization. It is an existential threat to humanity. The format of this section is to discuss the origin of the legal profession and its role in society. Then we discuss the expected role of lawyers in our USA society, and then we discuss my lawyer, the origin of Don-got-me lawyers, and how Americans should deal with Don-got-me's. We conclude with our wish for conversion of Don-got-me's and how the government could help by banning Don-got-me ads on TV and in print.

Lawyers in the USA

No country in the world has as many lawyers per capita as the USA. There is one for every eleven people per a former English barrister now living in the USA. Google states that there are about 1.3 million lawyers in the USA for a US population of 320 million. Thus, per Google, the number is one lawyer for every 248 people. In China, the rate is one for every 450,000 people. In Mexico it is about zero for whatever their population is. (I tried to hire one for a land purchase. I could not find a single lawyer in the Yucatan peninsula). The USA is a country brimming with lawyers. When and how did this situation start?

The concept of a lawyer goes back to English Common Law. Someplace in antiquity in England a set of laws was established for their society. The laws were their "thou shall not do this" and apparently the written laws needed interpretation to be administered to control their society, and lawyers arose to meet the need.

A lawyer was a person who understood the laws that governed a society and interpreted them for a fee for people needing legal help.

Sounds noble. Sounds like a good thing. How did they spill over into the USA?

English Common Law lawyers existed well before the USA. The USA started in 1781 with the Articles of Confederation. Thirteen states became a sovereign nation. Each state was also a sovereign nation at that time. Each had a governor and legislature, even an army (militia). However, during the revolution, the people living in the thirteen states decided to take all of the land that the King of England took from the indigenous people, the people who lived in the Americas for thousands of years. There is nothing to be added to this discussion in arguing the ethics of events that produced the USA from land owned by others, but it happened.

The constitution was written by a group of leaders from the thirteen states. Some were well-to-do business people, some were farmers, and some were people who were proficient in English common law. Much of the US Constitution was crafted by a well-schooled wealthy person by the name of James Madison. He wanted a limited government and one free of factions (like farmers versus merchants). He also wanted the states to keep their states as mini-nations. The state's best know the needs of their residents.

The way that the constitution created the need for lawyers was that each aspect of the constitution that produced a law needed interpretation. Also, the constitution created a court that would be above all of the courts that existed in the sovereign states; the Supreme Court. This court was to be above all of the state courts. This solution did not work very well when people from New York and Georgia had to deal with the Supreme Court in Washington D.C. Thus, appeals courts evolved sometime before the Civil War and this movement spread around so that state issues and federal issues could be resolved in area appeal courts and only really exceptional cases had to be resolved by the Supreme Court.

Lawyers, as we know them, started as a profession in England. People became lawyers in the newly formed USA by being schooled in the USA's federal, state, and local laws and offered their services for a fee. State licensing of lawyers did not start until about 1840. President Lincoln was a lawyer, but he may not have had a license from the

State of Illinois as would now be required. Now to practice law in the USA you have to pass a state exam (bar exam) and pay an annual fee to a state for your license.

As laws became more complex, lawyers became specialists in certain areas. Some lawyers specialize in analyzing legal contents, some deal with real estate, some deal with marital issues, some deal with treaties with other countries etc.. Trial lawyers are lawyers that have sufficient skills to deal with the complications of jury trials. In auto insurance cases, 94% of claims are settled without a jury trial. Personal injury lawyers have developed specialized skills to deal with insurance company lawyers and juries.

Don-got-me lawyers are a rogue branch of trial lawyers. They have special schooling in how to overcome and defeat insurance company lawyers. We will discuss them in a separate section.

My Lawyer

This book may appear to paint lawyers in a negative light. That is not our intent. In fact, "my lawyer" has always been considered to be a family friend. Early in my engineering career, we built a new house for my wife and two sons. We needed a lawyer in my state to check out the details of the property that we were purchasing. My mother-in-law knew a person who had a lawyer that she liked and so we hired him to close on the new house that we built. A few years later we bought a small house nearby to rent to my parents. Their big house in the city became surrounded by homes that were not properly cared for. The area went from lovely community to dangerous slum. They had to get out. We rented the little house in the suburbs to my parents and "our lawyer" took care of the purchase, rental agreements and even legal matters for my parents. "Our lawyer" was a big part of our family. When our three sons (we added one after building our new home) were all in school my wife decided to buy more small houses and rent them to help family finances. Our lawyer was involved in each house purchase and rental agreements. We got to know his wife and family. He even did what was needed to get money from renters who slipped away in the night. So, for two decades or so "our lawyer' took care of all of our legal needs. When he died, still young by most standards, his stepson who was also a lawyer, became "our lawyer". He had been handling our property, will and LLC issues and every legal matter until the Disney accident scam. He told me that he did not want to get involved in the personal injury, Don-got-me scenario. I was without a lawyer for the first time in fifty-five years.

The Origin of Don-Got-Me Lawyers

Some people (not me) claim that they crawled from under a rock. I do not know if they have their own society, like trial lawyers, but they may have some kind of secret society where they share intelligence about the competency of insurance company adjustors and investigators.

However, there may be no intelligence there to be had. (Sorry, keep thinking about my insurance company).

It is my belief that Don-got-me lawyers evolved from honest trial lawyers. There is a lot to trial law that differs from all other law. You do not need to know anything other than how to convince twelve or so strangers that you are right and the other person is wrong. Law schools teach how to do this. They teach that you have to get control over a witness in the stand with "leading" questions, like: "Is your name Ralph?" He must say yes. The lawyer keeps asking questions like this for as long as possible then throws in "Did you cause this accident?" The person says "yes", as he had been directed. Police do this sort of thing in questioning suspects.

Lawyers are well schooled in psychology. They know about different behaviors, different personalities. They know what confuses people; they know how to make people believe things. They use their knowledge of psychological behavior to select candidates for a jury. I can talk with a stranger for five minutes and establish a psychological profile for that person. I can see their soul. It is a curse to me, but it is a gift that many trial lawyers possess. I have been called to jury duty many times, but I have never made it past a first lawyer interview. I suspect that my ability to see people's souls (and lawyer's intent) showed. I apparently was designated "not easy to convince". Don-got-me lawyers are lawyers that become skilled in selecting jurists that could be swayed in what they are purveying.

Trial lawyers are argumentative and adversarial. Our entire USA legal system is adversarial. In a trial, a plaintiff (the person seeking money) competes with the defendant (where the money will come from) and so do their lawyers. Some people have never lost their primeval instinct to take the kill from the other wolves. They do not want to share. They want the entire kill. I have been a yacht club member for most of my life and racing has been a priority for most of the yacht club members. They are not satisfied with a nice sail; they need to go faster than other boats to show their superiority and strength over others. They want the whole kill. All humans are born with a brain consisting of two parts, the conscious and the nonconscious. Cognition is a product of the conscious brain. Animal instincts, like self-preservation, are products of the nonconscious brain. Competition (taking the whole kill) comes from the nonconscious brain as do accident fraud, rape, murder and the like. There are no laws in the nonconscious brain. There is only "self" (him or herself).

Trial lawyers want to win. They are competitors. They may not get paid if they do not win. That is often the situation with Don-got-me lawyers. No win, no millions, no Lexus. Don-got-me's are lawyers who demonstrated to themselves and to insurance company lawyers that they will win. Do not try to challenge me. Every individual athlete has developed his or her secrets to winning. I was a competitive back stroker in high school and college. My secret to winning was cheating. I have some kind of funny bone situation in my feet that makes a big bone stick out on the side of my feet. My funny-shaped wide feet acted like swim fins that I used to defect swimmers with normal feet. My physical deformity worked best on the backstroke.

Don-got-me lawyers may use a personality trait to beat the competition. For example, one Don-got-me ad where I live shows him having lunch with his mother, and talking with children to create the illusion that he is the honest nice person down the street. He wants juries and clients to think that he is not the kind of person who would coax accident victims into fraudulent injury claims or that accident anguish is worth a settlement of fourteen million dollars.

Don-got-me lawyers are likely lawyers who developed significant skills in arguing any assigned topic. They have no concern for the right or wrong of something. A good Don-got-me lawyer could argue that rape is a good thing and his client was performing a public service.

Showmanship and ego are usually part of Don-got-me "lawyership". They tend to put themselves in front of all others in their TV ads. They love their huge face on everybody's screen. They boast how insurance company lawyers quiver in their presence. They are easily beaten down. They are really not equal competitors. The mandatory part of their TV advertisements is to show healthy good looking young people who smile because "Don got me 2.5 million and as you can see, I am healthy and whole and I did not have to do anything to get my 2.5 million other than say I have distress or some other 'malady' that cannot be measured by any medical or scientific method".

What society expects of lawyers

What is so disconcerting about Don-got-me's is that they are prostituting their profession blatantly on TV and on billboards. Suppose medical doctors went on TV and promised "come to me and I will cure your cancer." Drug companies do this, but they are of the same ilk as Don-got-me's. What Don-got-me's are doing is the same as advertising fentanyl to teenagers as a way to become popular within your social group. My father-in-law suffered more that I can imagine from a hospital mistake. He became a quadriplegic. For thirty years he was confined to a wheelchair and had to be fed and washed and everything by my wife's family. Fortunately, there were six children to help. My father-in-law was a civilian employee of the US Airforce during World War II. He got a hernia on the job and a base doctor operated to fix the hernia. He was given a spinal anesthetic by a military doctor against his wishes in a military hospital and he slowly lost movement in his arms and legs and within four months he was a quadriplegic. He could never work again. He could not sue. It was wartime, and you cannot sue the military. The federal government paid his medical expenses, but my mother-in-law had to become the breadwinner for a family of eight. There were no 2.5 million awards for anguish.

Don-got-me lawyers typically get $300,000 awards for fabricated injuries.

Injuries that cannot be medically measured (like trauma) are the basis for the "Don-got-me business.

This is the outright crime that Don-got-me's commit and brag about it on billboards. Lawyers have to have sufficient intelligence to make it through college and pass the bar. They full well realize that they are making fraudulent injury claims. They full well realize that showing healthy people in their ads gives the message that "you can sue for millions even though you have no real injuries." Don-got-me's known how to befuddle insurance company employees and shower non-injured people with riches beyond imagination.

The United States cannot survive as a nation when its entire population is exposed to incessant indoctrination that faking an injury (embellishment of something in one's mind) will make you rich. My biggest expense, more than taxes, food, clothing, hospitalization and housing, is the cost of insurance (health, auto, home, liability, boat, etc.) Giving millions and billions to Don-got-me lawyers raises the cost of insurance to all. Brainwashing people to sue for manufactured injuries is the height of dishonesty in my opinion.

Americans deserve a legal system free of dishonest law suits. Don-got-me's know that there is not a mechanism to stop what they are doing. What they are doing is lucrative. A Don-got-me in my city claims that his firm has gotten billions from insurance companies. Nobody will ever start a company or do anything because each and every American now lives with the constant fear that Don-got-me's will take everything that they have. Like they did to me.

Summary

The lawyer dilemma is that USA's legal system is so complicated that lawyers are needed to cope with our laws in general. We need lawyers that we can trust to guide us around legal issues, but there is a cadre of lawyers that are competitive and gifted in trial work who are superior to any insurance lawyer and they can continue to convince anybody who is involved in any way with an automobile collision to sue for millions if not billions. They preach:

Never, ever say that you are not hurt in a collision. Any collision causes permanent injury. We can convince any jury. They are putty in our hands.

By my estimate, every city in the USA that has a TV station will have three to twenty Don-got-me's. We even have a Donna-got-me in my city. There are about 2000 TV stations in the USA with an average of ten Don-got-me's per city and they preach suing for "any injury". They are indoctrinating most of America's population that suing for no real reason is a guaranteed path to wealth. Suing is much better than the lottery. And this is an existential problem for America.

Chapter 10
Solving the Don-got-me problem
The problem

Every USA city has a cadre of Don-got-me lawyers and they advertise incessantly on TV and billboards. They offer a lottery-like windfall for faking a lifelong injury. The TV and billboard ads show happy, healthy smiling people with no visible impairments. Of course, it could be that those lawyers suggested immeasurable maladies to their clients, such as:

>stress
>
>anxiety
>
>mood disturbance
>
>sleep difficulties
>
>trauma
>
>distress
>
>discomfort
>
>unhappiness
>
>etc.

A mentioned in an earlier chapter, my city of residence handed out four million dollars to a Don-got-me lawyer, because a city firefighter became "uncomfortable" because he was offered Kentucky Fried Chicken at a Juneteenth party.

The last manufacturing company is being reduced to nothing by a cadre of Don-got-me's suing the company over ear plugs that did not keep out all of the noise.

There is no end to the absurdity of Don-got-me lawsuits. However, the United States cannot survive the next decade unless something is done to curb the Don-got-me's. The damage is to all US citizens and the net result will be no businesses, no manufacturing, no medical professionals, no anything; the US will be home to 15 million lawyers with nobody to provide services to them: Armageddon.

It is the purpose of this chapter to explore available options to solve the Don-got-me problem. Of course, the chapter objective is to identify solutions that could possibly work. We will start by pondering a lawmaker-generated solution; then medical intervention, then ethics, then shaming, finally we will discuss what we used to deal with world annihilation in the 1950's: conversion (it was the USSR at that time).

Legislative help

This is the most doable solution to the Don-got-me problem. We have a precedent. Lawyers like precedents. Laws could be formulated at the federal and state levels to ban Don-got-me advertising. We used to have such a ban in the USA on so-called "hard alcohol". TV ads are not permitted on liquors and wines. The reason is obvious. There are millions of alcoholics who have had their lives destroyed by addiction to alcoholic beverages. Why beer ads are permitted is another absurdity. More people are addicted to beer than to liquor. It is cheaper and easier to consume in public, but it is just as destructive.

Lawmakers at appropriate levels could copy the laws that limited liquor advertising and apply these to Don-got-me's. I do not know what the state or federal penalties are for advertising liquor, but whatever they are, they seem to be effective. The law must be effective, since I never met a person addicted to "hard stuff", however, I know of many lost lives due to beer. The lost lives from driving under the influence of alcohol in the USA are staggering. The persons who have "died in DWI accidents" from beer addiction is significant. Thus, advertising an evil can multiply that evil many times. It costs every driver in the USA at least $500 in increased insurance costs and with 100 million insured drivers, that is an annual cost of 50 billion dollars. The loss of life is significant. I lost my trust in institutions to an accident fraud with a Don-got-me accomplice. There may be no words to describe the Don-got-me evil adequately. I personally have seen at least one million TV ads and 400,000 billboards advertising a lifetime of wealth if you sign on to injury fraud with a Don-got-me.

Besides banning Don-got-me ads on TV, billboards, print, and on-line, legislators could make laws limiting accident liability to payment of medical expenses or burial costs. Take the example of the bus driver who faked a back injury from his fabricated sideswipe video. If there had been a way to present my case to a judge and jury, I could show the world how the criminals carried out their scam. I spent more than six hundred hours analyzing the fraudulent videos, but I was never allowed by my insurance company to present this information to anyone. It would be really nice if the State of Florida had an accident fraud function that I could have petitioned. Florida made fabricated accident videos a felony with no law enforcement agency charged with prosecution of the crime.

A solution would be for the State of Florida to have an accident fraud function with a staff charged with prosecuting things like fraudulent accident videos. Florida and all state lawmakers should formulate legislation taking the license to practice away from Don-got-me lawyers who know that they are participating in a fraud. This is incontrovertible in my case. Lawyers are not dumb. They can be evil, but not dumb, or they would not have made it through law school. Any person with sufficient intelligence to finish high school and earn a living knows that a sideswipe of a 40,000-pound vehicle by a 2800-pound vehicle cannot produce a life altering injury in the bus driver. Such side forces do not cause lifelong disabilities on bus or truck drivers. Thus, the Don-got-me lawyer unquestionably is an accomplice in the bus driver fraud. If a viable accident fraud law was in place he would be disbarred.

In summary, law makers at every level could develop laws to stop Don-got-me frauds and offering the public huge sums of money for participating in accident fraud (mostly faked injuries). Substantial punishment of "accident victims" in frauds would also be helpful. My brother-in-law hit a vehicle with three people aboard. They all got $300,000 injuries. None got more than bruises. There was no ambulance called. Apparently, the Don-got-me lawyer knew that he could claim $300,000 damages without question by anyone. This is the system that needs to be legislated away. A medical review board consisting of at least three practicing physicians should be required to verify injuries in any legal accident injury claim with signed avadavats.

I got sued for $300,000 for alleged injuries to the driver of the bus that rear-ended me. The notice of claim had a few medical terms like low back injury and may need surgery. It sure would be nice if "injured" parties had to verify injuries with medical reports from approved medical professionals that must be supplied to the party being sued, like me. I recently went shopping for a new doctor to perform a significant and difficult operation on me. To go shopping I needed a complete and substantive medical record of my condition and the need for the surgery. My current doctor was too old (seventy-six) to perform the surgery that he recommended. I went shopping with 40+ pages of detail on my condition.

If there was any kind of justice involved in the Don-got-me industry I would have been given the medical records citing the injury and how it was caused by a side swipe from three medical professionals whose names and resumes were available to me and to publish as public record.

Certainly an affidavit with penalties for perjury should have been supplied to me for my accident fraud. I would love to see in writing a legal statement from the bus driver explaining how a falsified side swipe produced a $300,000 injury in him. I spent a half hour with him after he rear-ended me and he was fliting in and out of the bus, moved it all over creation. Then he dashed back to the bus and drove off in hit and run mode. He did not give me his insurance details or even his name and address.

The lure of lottery-like winnings causes people to make false accident claims and if they were required by law to document that their injuries are real by statements from at least three medical professionals, this would go a long way in suppressing Don-got-me activity.

Medical intervention

Don-got-me disease is a mental illness on the part of the Don-got-me lawyer. All fraudulent lawsuits are the product of mental illness. All human activity is produced by the human brain. As mentioned previously, there are two parts to every brain: the conscious, which an individual controls and the nonconscious which is controlled by a person's DNA and molecular makeup. The nonconscious brain is 90% or thereabouts of the brain and we humans only carve out consciousness from the nonconscious brain to differing degrees. The nonconscious brain controls the autonomous nervous system and related functions. It is part of the self-preservation component in our genes and DNA. Humans are born thinking only of themselves. Babies cry when they want servicing. They want food and to be comfortable. Their nonconscious brain is controlling things.

Don-got-me lawyers are allowing (encouraging) their nonconscious brain to control their lives. The Don-got-me life produces wealth and the nonconscious brain likes wealth and to be fed and made comfortable. Their "id" is in control of their life and lawyering business. There is a problem with the brains of the Don-got-me lawyers. They need constant attention and money.

This is a mental health issue. Don-got-me lawyers are allowing the nonconscious, uncaring for others, part of their brain to be in control. It is like a drug or alcohol addiction. The conscious part of their brain is not carrying out conscious behavior. Just as psychologists and psychiatrists have developed medical cures for troubled minds, so could they also treat Don-got-me's. These are severely troubled people. They care not about destroying lives; they care not about truth and justice; they only care about awards for whatever. If they can lure someone into the lawsuit inferno their nonconscious brain, which is without morality, is in control.

Psychiatrists may have treatments available for Don-got-me's. They know to their core that what they are doing is wrong and evil by any standards, yet they do it because it pays well. They will rot in hell for it, but their damage to humanity could be ameliorated with medical intervention. Just as AA offers a path to sobriety, there could be counseling and drugs to cure Don-got-me's. Please Pfizer work on a pill to cure Don-got-me.

Ethics

How about Don-got-me's curing themselves? Most professions have codes of ethics. In engineering, licensing requires that engineers practice their profession in accordance with a set of guidelines that ensure public safety as well as the personal integrity of the engineers. Medical professionals similarly have a code of ethics to govern their personal and business behavior. For example, they do not advertise on TV or billboards discount surgery. They (most) do not do unnecessary medical procedures. Many professions, even elected officials in the USA, are "governed" by a code of ethics.

Ethics is a euphemism for abiding to the" ten commandments". We all know what they are and whatever their origin or authorship they are guidelines that are necessary for a civilization to exist and to sustain itself. You should not lie, cheat, steal, kill or take your neighbor's wife without consent. Honor your father and mother. Do not covet other people or their stuff etc. The 10 "commandments" are common sense. You cannot live in a community if the community leadership is taking tax money and using it for personal uses.

Ethics should be instituted into the legal profession. Lawyers have professional societies. It would be wonderful if these societies established codes of ethics for lawyers and a way to establish conformity. Certainly Don-got-me's are incommensurate with any ethics or commandments and even common sense. They should never be allowed by their profession to get four million dollars for offering a person a KFC wing and thigh. They need to be censured. Sure, they can do it. A cunning lawyer can select a dense jury that will award millions for a fried chicken offer. People can be putty in the hands of a non-ethical Don-got-me.

If the law profession wanted to become an asset to life on the planet, they would establish a code of ethics that, among many other things, establishes limits on Don-got-me's. Don-got-me's should be ruled unethical and lawyers who do Don-got-me should be disbarred and removed from professional lawyer societies.

Shunning

I recently toured a section of the USA that was heavily populated by a religious sect that opts not to waste their time on the planet with electric gadgets and unnecessary machines. They farm for a livelihood and use animals for their designated purposes. I was told by the bus tour leader that if one of their members stops observing their traditions they can be shunned. They can be left out of the group's traditional activities. I do not know the specifics, but I was told that this was an effective way to get followers to keep traditions in place.

Would it be possible to solve the Don-got-me problem by shunning the Don's? We know who they are. They like to show themselves in the TV ads. Of course, they are an object of derision on the part of reasoning people, but to the people who cannot resist their lottery-like award for nothing, they are a means to personal wealth and they love them. If the people who personally know the Don's start to shun them and their evil and unethical behavior, this may do more than a code of ethics in modifying their behavior. Wives and husbands should withhold sex. Parents should stop watching their kids and feeding them on holidays. They should be denied membership in all golf clubs and any other organization that operates with good intentions.

Children of Don-got-me lawyers should be ashamed of their parent or parents who participate. Neighbors know who the Don-got-me's are. They should shun the Don and his family. Shunning does not cost money and it can be an effective tool in showing Don-got-me's that what they are doing is wrong, evil, and incommensurate with living in a community.

Conversion

How about all of us pray for the conversion of Don-got-me's? We did this in my Catholic school in the

1950's to convert the Soviet Union. They were a god-less society trying to impose slavery on all others on the planet with them as the slave holders.

Our prayers worked, and President Reagan got the Soviet Union to break-up. Russia is repeating a world take-over, but this time they enlisted the Russian Orthodox Church to try and negate the prayers of the free world for the return of conscience to Vladimir Putin.

When individuals become so consumed by their nonconscious brain that they cannot even make a reasoned decision, prayers may be the only answer.

We in the USA are in a Don-got-me epidemic. The TV ads are so numerous and constant that it makes turning on the device an action akin to a prefrontal lobotomy. How can anybody continue to endure these people? They have no soul. Prayers may be the only way to keep Vladimir Putin from destroying Planet Earth, prayers may be necessary to solve the Don-got-me problem. Forgive them Father; they know what they are doing and do not care.

Honesty

Honesty is an acquired behavior. Babies are not born recognizing that something may belong to another. Babies together, each with their "own" things, will take each other's things. They have not learned the concept of ownership. All humans are born with a gene-controlled need for self-preservation. The baby wants every need fulfilled.

There is no concern for others; another baby nearby is a competitor to be dealt with by aggression when the other baby infringes on baby one's things or territory. This is the animal instinct produced by our autonomous or non-conscious brain. Honesty is a product of our conscious brain.

Don-got-me lawyers are still in "id" mode. They know when a person is faking an injury, yet they go ahead and steal with fraudulent lawsuits. They have become intrinsically dishonest. They do this because of a similar behavior/conscience flaw: greed. They make one-third at least of all fraudulent claim settlements. This makes them wealthy; they can acquire more and more possessions; more fraud, more income, more possessions.

What can be done to impart honesty in Don-got-me lawyers? How about belief in the tenets of Christianity like belief in the Ten Commandments? The Ten Commandments are not really religious in origin. They are the unwritten covenants between people to make civilization possible. Psychologists have studied primitive tribes living apart in jungles, as they have for millennia. They learned that these tribes with no outside influences kill each other, steal, share women etc. They cannot have a civilization. That is why after about 10,000 years they have not progressed from hunter/gatherers in a small tribe. Nobody tempered their "id"; they are controlled by their nonconscious brain; they are still in self-preservation mode.

I learned about the conscious and nonconscious brain through DVD courses taught by distinguished professors of psychology, neurology, molecular biology and medical professionals. Individuals do not control their autonomous brains. It is what keeps the heart pumping, the lungs oxygenating blood; it is when we are in nonconscious behavior like sleep. A person can deal with his or her nonconscious brain by carving out cognition and making it part of our conscious brain. Don-got-me lawyers could learn to add honesty to their conscious brain and to refuse the dishonesty cravings for their nonconscious brain. How do you do this? The nonconscious brain can be altered into conscience behaviors by repetition. Being honest in one small thing after another can carve out honest behaviors as a part of one's operating system. Honesty had to be carved out of the nonconscious brain the same as murder of others had to be carved out. The person still in "id" does not consider killing others wrong or taking the possessions of others wrong. Don-got-me lawyers need to reflect on the working of their brain and decide if they need to carve out honesty as a behavior; they need to temper their "id".

An exercise that could be used to carve out honesty from the nonconscious brain is for the Don-got-me lawyer to think about the earthly possession that they like best of all. Then think about someone (like the IRS or other super-powerful entity) taking that away forever. Each day do this with another possession. Keep doing this as long as it takes to carve out honesty in their conscious brain. Every time that they win a fraudulent case like mine, they are stealing others' possessions. Hopefully, thinking daily about how someone from out of nowhere takes their beloved possessions may impart some quantity of honesty into their conscious brain.

It is also recommended that Don-got-me lawyers meditate daily on what they are doing to civilization when they advocate daily on TV and billboards that they can bring riches to healthy people if they fake injuries or some form of trauma. A mantra will help. Here is a suggested one:

I know that I can select a jury to convict anybody of anything and I can use this power for good or evil.

A half-hour meditation in the morning and before bed will likely have the most benefit. It is difficult to carve honesty from the nonconscious brain. It is really, really difficult when the dishonest lawsuits provide so many wonderful worldly possessions. We love our mansions; we love our exotic cars; we love our pampered lifestyle. Meditation can serve to question our valuation of possessions, fame and fortune.

Reflection

In my incident, the Don-got-me lawyer participated knowingly in the theft of a large sum of money from an insurance company comprised of employees who process cases for a living with the thought process that grocery checkout cashiers give to a can of beans. Here is a claim; I get paid if I pay it or deny it. Paying is less bother. The Don-got-me's knowing their prey. They believe that insurance company investigators are absolute dunces and no match for their skills.

Similarly, Don-got-me lawyers know full well that a bus driver of a 40,000-pound full-size sixty-passenger bus does not receive any noticeable change in trajectory when side swiped by a 2900-pound car. So how would the bus driver get injured by a side swipe? Of course, there was no side-swipe. It was something concocted by the bus company and the insurance investigator. I was rear-ended. I was stopped and rear-ended by the bus, but nobody will listen or look at my evidence.

The Don-got-me lawyer never asked how his client was injured. He accepted the thief's statement that he injured his back and he may need surgery. This is probably the highest point in the lack of honesty and deceit in their daily dishonesty. The Don-got-me's have no soul; they have no ethics; there are no adjectives to describe how Don-go-me's subvert their lives to pure evil.

What is going on in Don-got-me lawyer's minds when they solicit the public endlessly to come forward and commit a crime that pays well? Do they concentrate on the twelve million judgments that will shut down a car repair company that for thirty years employed at least ten people for that time? Do they think about the life that was lost (mine) by participating in an obvious fraud? How do Don-got-me's sleep? How can they quell their mind to allow the unconsciousness needed for rest?

How do the Don-got-me's have a family? How can they look a child or even any other person in the eye, knowing what they do for a living? Apparently, the money to be made in the suing business over-rides the mental controls that normally governs civility, right versus wrong and living in a civilization. Nothing in life matters, except money and winning over those who are weaker. Primal instincts reign.

I feel like the five or so Don-to-me's in my hometown are part of my everyday existence. I habitually watch the local and national news on free TV. The leading Don-got-me's in my city come on every minute or so in both news sessions asking healthy people to claim injury in any "accident". An out of town Don-got-me has recently tried to weasel into the city-wide business. They finally found a person with a limp to show as a genuine injury. However, the two leading Don-got-me's continue to show strong, young, healthy people claiming "Don got me 2.5 million (and there is nothing wrong with me)".

A Miracle

We humans have but a femtosecond of life in the spectrum of time. Eighty or even ninety years is nothing to a planet that is billions of years old in a universe that is even older. Does what we do with our femtosecond matter? Does anything that living creatures do matter? For whatever the reason, humans tend to have beliefs that guide their behaviors during their femtosecond. Beliefs and behaviors reside in the conscious brain. Evil animal instincts and Don-got-me behavior reside in the nonconscious brain - the soulless portion of our existence. The portion of the brain that would make us cannibals and eat our offspring for self-preservation.

A miracle is needed to stop the Don-got-me's and this book could be the vehicle for one miracle at a time. If one Don-got-me reads it and converts that will be miracle. Ridding a metro area of its Don-got-me's will be a mega miracle.

Changes to the rules governing lawyers may produce country-wide conversion. It seems far-fetched but America is at stake and a miracle is needed. The United States of America cannot continue to exist when its lawmakers concentrate on lawsuits over fried chicken, lawsuits over any new product, lawsuits over everything, lawyers telling the public that they can be made rich by saying that they are hurt in any and all accidents. Hurt could mean occasional sadness or negative feelings, or uneasiness – all things that cannot be medically measured. A hurt back cannot be measured. A sad feeling cannot be measured. Yet Don-got-me's get juries to award millions over such things.

Hopefully one lawyer at a time will read this petition for sanity and stop their destructive, dishonest and damning behavior. Hopefully Don-got-me's will ponder the value of their ill-gotten wealth in the meaning of life. Hopefully they will be able to empathize with the victims (me) created by their fraudulent accident injury lawsuits.

Maybe the 600 or so elected officials who control the USA will recognize the existential nature of the Don-got-me lawyer problem and propose legislation for every legal entity in the USA outlawing contingency lawsuits. My bus driver had absolutely nothing to lose by lying about what happened. He did not have to pay for a lawyer. Similarly his Don-got-me lawyer had nothing to lose. He spent 15 minutes on paperwork to the insurance company for his third of a $60,000 award. Contingency lawsuits are causing the loss of civilization. Everybody sues everybody because there are no risks and the potential windfalls are staggering.

Contingency lawsuits should be outlawed by our legislators.

Maybe law schools will start to screen candidate students based upon their ability to accept ethics and morality and place honesty before all other behaviors. Something must happen. Don-got-me's are proliferating like the Covid-19 pandemic in 2020. Every time I watch TV more show up. On a recent trip to several large US cities, I saw more Don-got-me billboards than trees. America cannot exist with runaway Don-got-me behavior on the part of its legal profession. And this is the message of this book.

Epilogue

This epilogue is an attempt to give adulation to the conquering heroes, the people who stole money from an insurance company and ruined a person's life. The victors are:

1. The bus driver who rear-ended a stopped vehicle and turned his negligence into a $60,000 gift from a clueless insurance company. (He asked for $300,000; he got a reduced settlement from the insurance company).
2. The bus company who fabricated a twenty-six second video that was so perfect that in the first viewing convinced an entire insurance company of 30,000 employees that it was an authentic and unaltered product of a dash cam.
3. The insurance investigator who refused to investigate.
4. The insurance company supervisors who refused to investigate the investigator's lack of investigation.
5. The insurance company CEO who has no concern over paying money to accident frauds.
6. The entire staff of Disney Corporation from security guard to CEO who successfully ignore public safety and treat their customers with contempt.
7. Florida law enforcement agencies who successfully used the "jurisdiction" weapon to allow auto accident scams to flourish.

8. The Don-got-me lawyers who initiated the entire scam through TV and billboard ads promising wealth for faked injuries.
9. The medical professionals who signed legal documents stating that a bus driver can be injured for life from a 30-pound sideways force on a 40,000-pound bus.
10. And last, but not least, the forty or so lawyers that I contacted about representing me. They all successfully turned me down because I refused to fake an injury (and faked injuries are their livelihood).

Parting message to the bus driver

You must be very proud to have successfully stolen $60,000 from my insurance provider. I hope that you pass along your acquired skill to your children. I hope that your wife is also very proud of you. You participated in a perfect scam. You cannot be prosecuted for your felony crime because the State of Florida had no identified state entity to enforce the statute against fraudulent accident reporting.

When you rear-ended me, I said to myself, "I hope he doesn't lose his job over this." Little did I know that your every move in the fraud was being directed by your bus-company employer. I hope that you have many more successful accident scams on Disney World property. It is perfect for scams, thefts, accidents and the like because no USA laws are enforced in Disney territory.

Suggestions to readers when confronted with a vehicle collision with a stranger are:

1. Never, ever, trust the other driver.
2. Call police immediately, but assume that they will not come.
3. Take photos of everything and if possible, record statements from the other driver and witnesses.
4. Get license plate numbers, names, addresses and phones numbers of the other driver and passengers and your passengers as well.
5. Do not exchange information unless a law enforcement officer is present to ensure that the other person's information is valid.
6. Never, ever claim that you were not injured. It may be delayed.
7. Try to call a lawyer at the scene for advice on how to proceed.
8. Photograph the scene, the road, the other people, the location, and get the GPS coordinates.
9. Never move your vehicle until completing the aforementioned steps.
10. If your vehicle is undriveable get the information on where it is being towed.
11. If other people in the incident claim injury, call ambulances and get the report from the first responder for every person. If they refuse to go to the hospital, they must sign a paper. Get a copy of this.

Parting message to the bus company

That is some company that you have. Your website claims locations in a dozen cities in Florida and that you have hundreds of buses to be chartered. Do you require all of your drivers to commit felony crimes or just the one who operates in Disney territory where no USA laws apply? The bus that rear-ended me was ferrying a family with small children eager for the Disney adventure. Does it not matter to you that your drivers are watching their cell phones while driving? (A phone on the bus dash was visible in one of your manufactured videos). How did your company acquire your expertise in doctoring dash-camera videos? You are good. You completely dazzled the "investigator" of my insurance company. Even though you submitted two different videos he declared both authentic and unaltered. I guess anything captured off TikTok and the like is sufficient for my insurance company, but I had to break your first video into 672 individual images to prove the fraud. Of course, my analysis was for naught, since my insurance company "investigator" never heard about "Photoshop" or the free on-line dash cam editing software. He believed unto death that videos from any electronic device cannot be altered. If a video can be sent in an email it is valid and unaltered.

What's next for your company? Will you have riders place their phone on a device that will send their credit card info from their phones? I wish you well in your criminal activities and I hope that any honest employees never have to participate in your accident scam program.

My suggestions to readers on selecting a charter bus company are:

1. Beware of companies who do not have a legitimate business address.
2. Do not ride on unmarked vehicles. If it is not covered with company advertising, something may be wrong.
3. Beware of bus drivers having a cell phone sitting on the dash or nearby (buckle up).
4. Do not charter a bus company without investigating who owns the company and how long they have been in business. Google them for customer satisfaction.
5. When hit by a bus with a dash cam ask for all details on recording and preventing alteration. Measure the location of the camera from the bus's vertical and horizontal centerline. Determine if they have a camera focused on the driver and passengers and get a copy of the company's procedure for use and loading of videos. How do they protect recorded videos from alteration?

I have had many bus rides since my fateful Disney accident and I noted if any had dash cams. Only one did. I asked the driver what his procedure for use was. He said that he only uses it

when in an accident or if some person on the bus falls. I asked him how he gets the video out. He showed me a USB port. He said it can be transferred to a laptop. I could not go further because he had very little knowledge of English. However, transferring video to a laptop is the perfect situation for Photoshop editing. I sure wish that my insurance company heard about Photoshop.

Parting message to my insurance "investigator"

I hope that you get professional treatment to resolve your seething hate for customers of your employer. I also hope that you find some employment in the future that does not involve contact of any sort with other people. I realize that working from home in pajamas does not help the formation of people skills, but you can take small steps to venture out. Maybe once a day leave your devices and walk a block or two around your neighborhood. When you see another person, force yourself to say good-day and smile. After several months of daily trips like this, try talking for a few minutes to another person, even your mother. After that, try to talk with strangers. Eventually you may develop the ability to communicate with others.

My suggestions to readers on discussing a collision to an insurance company "investigator" are:

1. Never, ever, talk with an insurance company "investigator", claims examiner, supervisor or any insurance company on the phone. Use email or letters only and keep copies of everything.
2. Never, ever, trust an insurance investigator.

3. If an investigator had questions, tell him or her to send a list and you will reply by mail.
4. Hire an attorney to reply to any insurance company queries. Give them only a written accident report.
5. Try to find a way to have an in-person contact with an insurance company over a claim.

Parting message to insurance company leadership

When I learned that I had been convicted of an accident by a fraudulent video that overwhelmed my "investigator", I tried talking with people at the insurance company who claimed to me to be supervisors and the like. I had phone conversations with these people and it was very clear that I was an annoyance and that I was to be dealt with accordingly. The insurance company leadership team responded "artificially" after each of my three letters to the insurance company CEO. My perception of these people was that they also worked from remote locations with each

in their pajamas with a dog barking in the background. There are no "offices" in the insurance company where people work together. Their only link is the company email address. None of these supervisors were in any way interested in viewing my evidence that showed their revered accident video to be a fraud. The fraud was accepted by the investigator on first viewing and that was final. I was convicted without due process.

My suggestions on dealing with insurance company supervisors and the like are:

1. Never, ever, talk with these people on the phone (only use email and letters).
2. Try to get an organization chart so that you know who you are dealing with.
3. Record everything that they communicate to you.
4. Do not trust them to be acting on your behalf.
5. Ask for statements that can be run through your lawyer.

Parting message to the insurance company CEO

Thank you for sending my petitions for help down the line. It did not help, but the fact that I heard from others in your company other than the investigator with personal problems was encouraging. After my first letter to you, I did not have to deal with him. I mostly dealt with a woman in Florida whose role in your company is still unknown to me.

Your Linked-in profile states that you were a lawyer by degree and thus I find it curious that you allow the Don-got-me lawyers to consistently overwhelm your company investigators and supervisors. They seemed to me to have absolute and total fear of questioning a claim from a Don-got-me. Google tells me that you cave in 94% of the time. You settle without a trial. If any vehicle collision ever needed to go to trial it was mine. I even prepared two PowerPoints (that I sent to you) for a jury trial. The only lawyer who was nice (and honest) enough to talk with me told me that insurance companies fear the cost of a jury trial that they will settle anything no matter how absurd (like the phony video) to avoid the cost of a trial. Insurance companies never defend their customers and Don-got-me lawyers know this. And this is why the Don-got-me lawyer problem is existential. It has continually expanded during my long life and it appears to be evolving into a situation where Don-got-me lawyers will be suing every institution and company out of business.

My suggestions to readers regarding insurance companies are:

1. Never assume that they are on your side; assume that they are adversaries. They are.
2. Never pay attention to the stupid TV ads that flood free TV. They are meaningless.
3. Select an auto insurance purveyor only on your parent's lifetime favorable experience. If you do not have parents go to Consumer Reports and the like.

Parting message to Disney Corporation

Your treatment of me on this issue and my safety issues that go back more than 20 years is like having Mickey beat Minnie in public. Disney World is not truly a happy place, but a place to exploit people. In the 1960's I regularly attended technical conferences in the LA area and I made it a point to go to Disneyland for lunch. At that time you could wander the park, but not go on rides for ten dollars a day. I enjoyed the sights and sounds and dining at one of the many restaurants. It was a happy place.

In the 1980's I acquired property near Disney World. For thirty-two years I visited Disney at least once per year. After the first ten years or so the park got "nasty". I mentioned how I could not leave when I wanted and how the road in or out could be barricaded at Disney's will. My last trip in 2019 was "horrible", up to a four-hour wait for popular rides. I took my granddaughter there for spring break in college. Disneyworld was an out of control "mosh pit".

The way that I was denied help on a scam operation on their property attests to the company becoming contemptuous of their customers. They got increasingly nasty. My letters to the CEO confirmed the company's demise to nastiness. I have no idea what made Disney mean, but the company's current demeanor is incommensurate with happy place.

My observations to readers about Disney Corporation's demeanor are:

1. People are not respected.
2. Public safety is not a concern of Disney. Check for entrance and exit closures.
3. Disney World being outside of USA laws makes the place a mecca for scams and the like. Beware and be alert when visiting. It is like the Wild West.

4. Pray for the conversion of Mickey and Minnie.

Parting message to Florida law enforcement

Never have I been so disappointed with any entity in my life as the State of Florida. They were no help in dealing with what they designated as a felony crime accident fraud. I cannot imagine why legislators pass laws without a designated entity to enforce the law. I must assume that Florida laws require self-enforcement. For example, I was told by some Florida law enforcement

Officer that the State of Florida requires a form to be filed on every auto collision in the state. I got the form, filled it out and sent it to the designated address at the state capitol. I never got an acknowledgement of its receipt and never learned of the purpose and objective of the procedure and what happens if you ignore the "law." Apparently, it does not relate to the problem at hand, determining who caused a collision.

Overall, I give the State of Florida law enforcement entity a resounding "F" for failure to serve and protect its citizens. Never in my life have I encountered such hostility, arrogance and unconcern. I never in my wildest dreams thought that I would encounter police officers who would leave a man beaten to near death by robbers and pass by on the other side of the road. Florida police use "jurisdiction" as their rationale for passing by. No police officer in the State of Florida is required to protect and serve a person or business outside of their jurisdiction and there is no way that a Florida resident or visitor can know what law enforcement agency responds to requests for help when they are in the time of need in the state.

There is no civilization without laws and means of enforcement. The State of Florida is participating in the existential threat of the Don-got-me lawyers by refusing to enforce their accident fraud law. They get paid whether they helped a person, saved a life, or not. I guessmost Florida Law Enforcement officers opt for "not". I really was shocked to see how I was rebuffed as I went up the line from city to county to state. There was unanimity: "not my job".

My suggestions to readers regarding use of law enforcement in a vehicle collision are the following:

1. Immediately call 911 and anticipate no uniformed officer to show at the collision scene.
2. Call a lawyer, they will turn you down, but at least you tried.
3. Only vote for candidates for public office who have specific actionable proposals to return peace, order and rule of law.
4. Buy an app for your cell phone that shows your law enforcement jurisdiction and phone number wherever you are.
5. Demand that your elected officials who control law enforcement require police officers to recite at daily role-call:

> "The citizens of (state the locality) pay my salary and should be listened to and treated with respect".

(PS: This will be tough. One time I asked an officer to investigate vandalism to my house. I found out who did it. He refused to investigate. I said, "Do you know that I pay your salary?" I barely escaped being pistol-whipped by a sergeant. Of course, he did not investigate.)

Parting message to the Don-got-me lawyers

You are a cancer on your profession. There are no words to describe how we the honest people (those of us who will not fake an injury) despise you. Your incessant advertising is a major lowering of the quality of life in the United States. Consumer Reports should rate areas of the country on "freedom from Don-got-me advertisement." I recently traveled a few hundred miles on the I-95 in Florida and counted over twenty Don-got-me billboards. You are destroying our physical environment as well as our mental well-being. The leading Don-got-me in my home city uses at least four full frontal ads during the half-hour evening news. If some psychology major did a study, he or she may find that the Don-got-me's are radicalizing young people to fake injuries.

Don-got-me's know that their radicalization of troubled minds works. The number of personal injury claims is rising exponentially. Don-got-me accident awards is the fastest growing industry

in the USA. Young minds are indoctrinated with the idea that instant wealth comes from claiming an unmeasurable injury, like anguish, from any accident. The ultimate example happened in my home city. A first responder got four million dollars from the city because he felt "troubled" when offered KFC chicken at a political event. The United States is beyond crisis level in people suing everyone and everything with deep pockets.

Lawyers are intelligent well-schooled people. They should be our country leaders, our elected officials, the portion of our society that keeps the society functioning. Instead, Don-got-me lawyers are pariahs. They are making innovation in any area impossible because an innovator will get sued out of existence with lawsuits on immeasurable injuries. Don-got-me's love the wealth and possessions brought on by their faked-injury lawsuits, but I suspect that few ponder the fact that they are only on the planet for a femtosecond in the spectrum of time and they will spend eternity paying for misuse of their talents during their femtosecond. Don-got-me lawyers need to deal with the meaning of life. You can put full frontal ads before the public every six minutes on TV, but will that give you the respect of your children or any real friends?

Our suggestions to readers of this book regarding Don-got-me lawyers are:

1. If you are in a collision call every Don-got-me that you can, and say, "I may be hurt. It's too early to tell."
2. If you make it through the AI interview, try to meet with the Don-got-me. Observe how they operate.
3. Pick the Don-got-me with the highest settlement offer.
4. Take the money stolen from the insurance company and give it to your favorite charity or the Ukrainian war effort. (At least some good can come from an evil.)

Parting message to the medical professionals who participate in medical fraud

How is "feeling uncomfortable" a personal injury worth four million dollars? This is the type of "injury" claimed in many Don-got-me lawsuits. Who are the medical professionals who prostitute themselves to allow the bus driver that rear-ended me to claim an injury? A helpful lawyer told me that lower back pain is the fool-proof injury to claim. You can go to a hospital and have a CAT scan, an MRI and all sorts of diagnostic procedures and there will always be something in the results that a medical professional can truthfully say could cause pain. Like chili, no two cooks make it the same; no lower back is the same.

I have had numbness in my right leg for ten years. My primary care physician tells me that it is probably due to some disk compression on my lower back. All humans have changes in disk height as they age. We all get shorter; that's life. Thus, there is a way to fake permanent injury even from a sneeze.

However, I was convicted by my insurance company of injuring the bus driver, and I was never shown any medical evidence, like a medical report. I saw on the notice of claim that the bus driver claimed lower back injury needing an MRI and possibly surgery. When the Don-got-me lawyer put "surgery", it signaled a phone call from two people from my insurance company who get involved with serious injuries. Of course, I know that the bus driver is faking an injury because there was no physical force event to create any injury. There was no impact. The bus had a huge rubber bumper and my vehicle was stopped on an angle. The bus pushed the car sideways. In addition, one of the many unedited and authentic videos submitted to the insurance company showed the bus driver getting up from his seat, going to the open door, looking both ways for traffic and going to talk with me. I was shown pulling a dangling rubber strip from my vehicle. I did this after the second time that I moved my vehicle to keep traffic moving.

I should have been given a legitimate medical report by my insurance company. A real medical report is something that states all details with regard to a medical condition. Last year I was told by my long-time urologist that I needed a special operation, a nephroureterectomy and he does not do this operation. I had to go shopping country-wide for someone to do this operation. I asked for a medical report from the hospital. I was given "garbage" twice, just reports of a few tests. I ended up contacting the hospital CEO. Then I received a medical report that allowed me to shop for a surgeon at the Cleveland Clinic and these kinds of institutions. There are insufficient medical reports and true medical reports. I received no information from my insurance company other than that the bus drive was seriously injured. Of course, he was not. Since the bus company owner lived in the Philippines, he may have gotten medical evaluations there by medical people who do not have the same standards and ethics as US medical professionals.

My suggestions to readers on injuries caused by a collision are:

1. Demand medical reports signed by medical professionals that are complete, understandable and fit for explanation to a jury.
2. To medical professionals who knowingly participate in injury fraud, may God forgive you?

The end of the nightmare

The United States of America is in a death spiral because of Don-got-me lawyers and related limitative entities that are parasites on the body of a nation. People cannot start businesses for fear of being sued. Large, hundred year old companies, like 3M are being dissolved by lawsuits that are absurd. We all know that "feeling uncomfortable" over being offered fried chicken did not produce a four- million dollar injury. Maybe it is time to eliminate the jury system. The Don-got-me's have perfected techniques to get juries to do whatever they want. Maybe it is time to mandate that government entities offer an AI or Watson trial prior to any jury trial. Both AI jury and IBM's Watson may not be swayed by Don-got-me techniques, theatrics and incentive frauds for paid liars.

What happened to me is so hard to believe; but it happened. There are companies that are run by people with no ethics, no morals, no honesty, only greed. There are individuals that can be swayed by Don-got-me promises for instant wealth; they will cede their soul to eternal damnation for money. We have law enforcement entities who get paid if they do nothing. We have large corporations like Disney and insurance companies that operate as a black hole. They do whatever they please and there is no way for customers or government agencies to question how they behave, how they treat their customers.

Then we have honest lawyers quaking in their boots at the thought of challenging the Don-got-me's. The overall message of this book is:

Don-got-me's and their ilk have convinced Americans that suing rather than working is the best path to wealth and a happy life. Elected officials could solve the Don-got-me problem by legislation to bar contingency lawsuits, or by mandating mediation for all vehicle accidents. The mediators could be public officials that do not fear the Don-got-me's. They could solve the problem with legislation that allows only settlements of reimbursement of medical expenses in any injury lawsuit. No four-million-dollar settlements for feeling uncomfortable. In any case, America must do something about the Don-got-me's or cease to exist. That is my opinion. This book is my opinion. I hope it stimulates action to solve America's litigation problem.